HANDEL AND THE OPERA SERIA

THE ERNEST BLOCH LECTURES—1

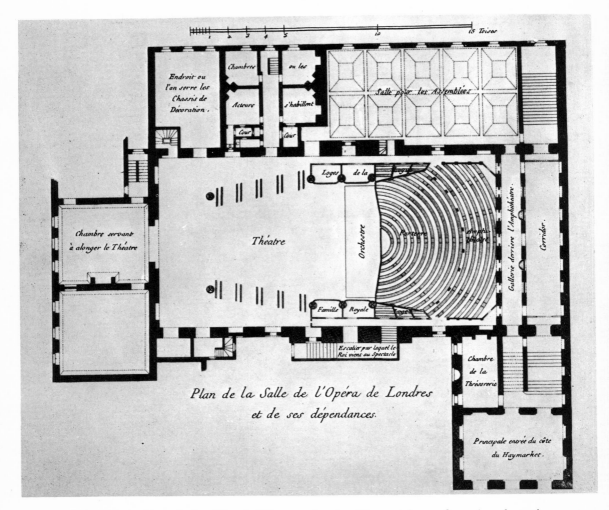

Ground plan of the King's Theatre in the Haymarket, after the alterations
of 1707–1708.

HANDEL
AND THE
OPERA
SERIA

WINTON DEAN

UNIVERSITY OF CALIFORNIA PRESS

BERKELEY AND LOS ANGELES

1969

University of California Press
Berkeley and Los Angeles, California

University of California Press, Ltd.
London, England

Copyright © 1969, by
The Regents of the University of California

SBN: 520-1438-3

Library of Congress Catalog Card Number: 79-78567
Printed in the United States of America

Designed by David Comstock

The Ernest Bloch Professorship of Music and the Ernest Bloch Lectures were established at the University of California in 1962 in order to bring distinguished figures in music to the Berkeley campus from time to time. Made possible by the Jacob and Rosa Stern Musical Fund, the professorship was founded in memory of Ernest Bloch (1880–1959), Professor of Music at Berkeley from 1940 to 1959.

THE ERNEST BLOCH PROFESSORS

1964	RALPH KIRKPATRICK
1965–66	WINTON DEAN
1966–67	ROGER SESSIONS
1968–69	GERALD ABRAHAM

to All My Friends in Berkeley

PREFACE

This book is based on the Ernest Bloch Lectures delivered at the University of California, Berkeley, in 1965/66. It deals with an extensive and sparsely charted tract of musical history, and should be regarded as a preliminary survey rather than a final assessment. I have tried to grasp the aesthetic issues raised by Handel's operas and to face the practical problems involved in their revival today. If they are to be more than beguiling curiosities, they must win their way in the theater. They are unlikely to prosper there unless their historical context is comprehensively studied and their virtues and drawbacks released from the obfuscation of prejudice and ignorance. Otherwise the labor of conductor, director, and singers, for all the temporary pleasure it may give, will not inaugurate a fruitful tradition.

The treatment of Handel in our musicologically oriented age has been strange. He was in his day the unrivalled master of opera and oratorio. Posterity placed his monument in the pantheon and hung this tribute round its neck, but omitted to examine the evidence on which it was based. Most of his works were buried, and it seemed that scholars were too much in awe of the monument—or perhaps too familiar with it—to disinter them. Until the last war no monograph on his operas or oratorios had been published in any language. The determining factor in the systematic revival of the operas that began in Germany in 1920 was not what Handel was attempting to express but what a modern audience was prepared to swallow. This criterion, though not everywhere paramount, still looms large. The more important question remains without a satisfactory answer. While the operas have inspired a number of articles in periodicals and learned journals, mostly on single works or aspects of Handel's style, there is no full study of them as living or potentially living art, conceived in terms of the theater and capable of eloquent speech in the modern opera house. They have been the subject of two books only, neither of which deals with the music. H. C. Wolff's *Die Händel-Oper auf der modernen Bühne* (Leipzig, 1957) is a brief pictorial summary of recent German revivals. Joachim Eisenschmidt's *Die szenische Darstellung der Opern G. F. Händels auf der Londoner Bühne seiner Zeit* (2 vols., Wolfenbüttel, 1940–1941), a doctoral thesis by a young German scholar killed in the last war, gives a very useful account of stage practice in Handel's London, but it scarcely begins to coordinate this evidence with that of the scores.

Nor have Handel's biographers, with the exception of R. A. Streatfeild [1] and Hugo Leichtentritt,[2] paid more than perfunctory attention to the operas. Edward J. Dent's survey,[3] while always stimulating and often penetrating, contains many odd judgments, governed perhaps by experience of the music on paper rather than in the theater. A challenging question mark still stands against Handel as a composer of opera. It has been my intention to remove it, and to demonstrate that the operatic phase of his career is not only of crucial importance for what followed, but offers a precious contribution to the stock of public pleasure available to lovers of opera.

It remains for me to make my peace with that "ombra cara," the mighty shade of the composer. In a study of the oratorios [4] I referred to the operas in terms that scarcely did them justice. What I wrote was accurate as far as it went. But further acquaintance with the scores and librettos, and above all with the operas in the theater, has convinced me that it did not go far enough. It left out of account the most important thing of all, the sheer genius that enabled Handel to overcome the limitations of his material and transmute an apparently decadent form into permanent art. This book will, I hope, make some amends.

[1] *Handel* (London, 1909; reissued New York, 1964).
[2] *Händel* (Stuttgart, 1924).
[3] In *Handel, a Symposium,* ed. Gerald Abraham (London, 1954).
[4] *Handel's Dramatic Oratorios and Masques* (London, 1959).

My thanks are due to Mr. Joseph Kerman for reading the type-script and picking some necessary holes; to the members of my seminar at Berkeley for throwing up a profusion of new facts and ideas; to Miss Sarah Ann Fuller for help in tracking down the sources of some of Handel's librettos; and to Mr. Philip Radcliffe for much stimulating discussion.

Contents

1 The Opera Seria Convention   1

2 Handel's Solution   17

3 Handel's Operatic Career   25

4 The Libretto   36

5 Heroic Operas   54

6 Magic Operas   77

7 Antiheroic Operas   100

8 The Craftsman in the Theater   123

9 Aria and Recitative   152

10 Orchestration   185

11 Modern Revivals   200

   General Index   215

   Index of Handel's Works   219

CHAPTER 1

The Opera Seria Convention

Larghetto.

Example 1

This exquisite melody may stand as a symbol of the fame and fate of Handel's operas over two centuries. It became celebrated throughout the English-speaking world as "Handel's Largo" (as if the tempo mark were unique), and enjoyed special favor as a voluntary for church organists. But it is not a sacred piece; it was not composed for the organ; it was not marked "Largo"; the musical germ from which it grew was not even composed by Handel, but by Giovanni Bononcini.[1]

[1] Harold S. Powers, "Il Serse trasformato," *Musical Quarterly* (Oct. 1961–Jan. 1962).

It is the opening arioso of Handel's opera *Serse*, a half-humorous piece sung by an oriental monarch (a soprano castrato) who is so misguided as to fall in love with a tree.

Handel's operas as a whole, until very recent times, have scarcely met with more comprehension. He was the greatest and most successful theater composer of his age, and he wrote more operas than any other composer of the first rank in any period. Yet for 160 years after his death they remained in the shadows. They were condemned out of hand as impossible and, apart from a few excerpts incongruously yoked to sacred or sentimental English texts, were never performed. Before 1955 few people outside Germany had seen or heard a Handel opera;[2] and most of the performances that had taken place, not least in Germany, deviated to a startling degree from anything Handel could have envisaged.

The position today is confused: neither total eclipse nor the blaze of noon. While most of the operas have been revived on the stage, some in several countries, none has attained the secure status of a repertory piece. In the opinion of a small but growing number of listeners many of them, if performed with sympathy and understanding, do work in the theater, not merely as a string of beautiful arias but as fully fashioned dramas obeying laws that may be unfamiliar but are consistent and fitted to their purpose. If this is so, the operatic repertory is not so rich in masterpieces that we can afford to go on ignoring them. Yet many musicians remain unconvinced, and perhaps the majority still regard Handel's operas as something between an outmoded social ritual and an artistic fossil.

The chief justification and reward of the musicologist is—or should be—not merely to investigate but to help in the process of re-creation, to make these dead bones live. If he continues to regard them as relics to be examined under a microscope or in a museum, dead bones they will assuredly remain. No music is alive until it is played. This applies particularly to opera, which has to be performed in two dimensions simultaneously, and most of all to opera in a lost or unfamiliar conven-

[2] An English Makropulos attending every stage revival between 1755 (when Handel was still alive) and 1955 could have heard three operas, each in a single production: not ten performances in all.

tion. Unless we can visualize Handel's operas in their full theatrical setting—and this involves understanding the conditions under which he worked, the conventions he accepted and shared with his audiences, and the manner in which he refined upon the practice of his contemporaries—it is not only impossible to enjoy them to the full, but difficult to grasp what they are about.

There are of course serious obstacles, practical and aesthetic, to be charted and overcome before a modern audience can accept Handel as easily as it accepts Verdi. In the first place a good deal of research is still needed to discover what Handel wrote, what he meant, and what he performed. There is no satisfactory printed text of most of the operas, and the greatest among them tend to be the least well served. Chrysander's edition, published in the nineteenth century, was a remarkable achievement for its time. But his scores of the operas leave much to be desired. They are often incomplete and inaccurate, ignoring autograph and other early manuscript material, confusing different versions, and taking little account of contemporary printed librettos with their insertions, cuts, additional and modified stage directions, and essential information about the plots.

These librettos are of great importance. They were the eighteenth-century equivalent of a program, complete with translation and cast list. They were also something very like a prompt copy for the stage director, who was the librettist himself (in London the adapter rather than the original author). This helps to explain why so much care was taken to keep the text up to date (including last-minute addenda and corrigenda at the end or on an inserted leaflet) and why a new edition was issued for almost every revival. They tell us a great deal of what the librettist–director intended in the way of stage movements, gestures, scene changes, and so forth. Chrysander's edition is often at variance with them; but it is difficult to distinguish between what he chose to ignore and what he failed to discover, since his prefaces are so laconic that they conceal far more than they explain. It is necessary to emphasize this, for the operas so far published in the new Halle edition[3] have been based not on the copious original sources but on Chrysander—

---

[3] Full score of *Serse*, vocal scores of *Ezio*, *Serse*, *Ariodante*, and *Giulio Cesare*.

with additional mistakes. The terrain of Handelian scholarship may be criss-crossed with ditches; but the bodies of the blind who have led each other into them scarcely offer a firm foothold to their successors.

Defective texts are only one barrier. A perfectly sound edition would still have to be translated into performance. There are many technical points involved (matters of notation, ornament, continuo realization, and so on) that cannot here be discussed in detail. They arise in all music of the period and are not peculiar to Handel, though their solution must of course take into account what can be discovered about his practice. All performers of baroque music are familiar with the problems, even if they do not agree about the answers. Since contemporaries do not seem to have been unanimous either, and there were ample opportunities for the exercise of individual taste—which was indeed one of the reasons why composers left the matter open—this is not a suitable subject on which to lay down the law, except in general terms. But if the operas are to yield up their secrets, they must be interpreted according to the style of their period by the conductor, the stage director, the designer of scenery and costumes, the orchestra, the continuo player, and not least the singers. There may be more than one right answer to each type of problem—that is a matter of taste. There are certainly a large number of wrong answers, and these have been prominent in modern revivals.

The aesthetic difficulties are as formidable as the practical. One of them was unwittingly created by Handel himself. The great oratorios of his last twenty years represent one of the peaks of the art of music. They have themes of universal application and grandeur, developed with as rich and intricate an organization as the Bach Passions or the music-dramas of Wagner. When we turn from them to the Italian operas of his earlier years, we are bound to feel an initial shock. So much of the Handel of the oratorios is missing: the English language of the texts; the noble simplicity of the stories from the Bible or classical mythology; the key position of the chorus, whether as dramatic agent or moral interpreter or merely as contrast; the flexible patterns in which solo and choral sections are interlinked so that we cannot predict the form of the next number. If we are to gain any understanding of the operas, it is essential that we avoid measuring them, consciously or tacitly, against the standard of the oratorios.

The Italian opera seria and the English oratorio represent absolutely distinct forms, composed in a different tradition, in a different language, for a different audience. The oratorio was a synthesis evolved by Handel himself and not bound by strict precedent. It was directed at a predominantly middle-class audience in their own language. It employed plots and sometimes whole texts that they had known since childhood, and drew part of its sustenance from the English choral tradition. The opera seria, defined by Dr. Johnson—not unfairly from the viewpoint of the average Englishman—as "an exotic and irrational entertainment," was a foreign import sung in a foreign language. It retained the aroma of its origins in the princely courts of Italy, and its audience was primarily aristocratic. It was bound by strong conventions that varied little throughout most of Europe, and was centered not on the chorus but on the solo voice. The subject matter of its plots was sophisticated, complex, and literary. Inevitably the artistic product of the two forms was very different. Any suggestion that Handel's operas are necessarily inferior, or superior, to his oratorios must prejudice inquiry from the start. One point however can be made with certainty: the listener familiar only with *Messiah* and *Israel in Egypt* will find in the operas whole facets of Handel's genius whose existence he could never have suspected.

The biggest problem, or series of problems, arises from the opera seria convention. The term "opera seria" is useful rather than exact; from time to time it has carried more than one shade of meaning, and certain types of humor have not always been excluded. If it is confined strictly to the "reformed" librettos of Zeno and Metastasio, we are left with no term for what they were trying to reform. Here it will be taken to cover all Italian opera other than opera buffa during Handel's life, which means virtually all opera outside France, for the insecurely established German and English schools were decaying from the first years of the eighteenth century. There were, as will appear, local variants within the Italian style, and Handel was to mix his own ingredients; but essentially the same conventions governed them all. These conventions are unfamiliar to a modern audience, except as facts in the history

books. The regular operatic repertory, from Gluck to Puccini and
Strauss, leads us to expect certain things to happen in an opera in certain ways. It is not easy to appreciate how selective a portion of the
experience of the past this represents. To accept a different dispensa-
tion, as we must if we are to enjoy Handel, may require a conscious
act of adjustment even from an intelligent audience before it can tune
to the right wave-length. Since this act of adjustment is the vital step,
it must be considered in some detail.

All art relies on convention, and opera more so than most, for it is
a synthesis of several arts. If the result is not to be chaos, there must
be a compromise, since each art—music, drama, scenery, costume, ballet,
stage machinery—will strive for supremacy. The form of this compromise varies from age to age, thereby constituting one of opera's chief
fascinations, but it is always highly artificial. Swans may sing before
they die, and other birds while establishing their mating territory, but
human beings normally do not; nor is an orchestra often available to
accompany their quarrels or their love scenes. Opera is also an intensely
social art. It is difficult to imagine an operatic performance without an
audience. And since it is and always has been an expensive as well as
a complex entertainment, its practitioners have to pay close attention
to the tastes of that audience, even—indeed particularly—when this
means obeying the whim of the autocrat who pays the bills. No modern audience can share the exact tastes of any audience of the past.
It is only when an artist, writing as he must in terms of his own time,
manages to transcend its particular compromise of tastes and conventions and communicates something we value today that we think it
worthwhile to keep his work in the repertory. In doing so we are making an act of adjustment.

Until the present century it was a commonplace of artistic as well
as of political and social thought that the passage of time and the gath-
ering of experience were steadily contributing to a wiser, maturer, and
more enlightened world. Wagner and his supporters thought he was
not only the latest thing in musical drama, which he was, but that he
had invalidated the methods and achievements of his predecessors, which
he had not. The idea that art progresses steadily upward has long been
exploded; but we are still coming to terms with the results of the explo-

sion, and it would be rash to assume that the process is complete. The late nineteenth century thought it had outgrown most of Mozart's operas, regarding *The Magic Flute* as childish and *Così fan tutte* as contemptible, and forgetting the existence of *Idomeneo*. Gluck was respected as Wagner's forerunner in cutting the singers down to size and abolishing the fripperies and trivialities of the old opera seria; but it was the reformer who was admired rather than the composer. Verdi, with the exception of his last two operas, where he was thought to have learned from Wagner, was condemned as primitive and vulgar. If the stars of these composers were in partial eclipse, that of Monteverdi had not been detected by the most powerful telescopes. If anyone thought of Handel's operas (except as a source of occasional pickings for the concert singer and even the church organist, with the spice taken out of the words and added in different form to the harmony), it was to condemn them as rudimentary in form and disfigured by an oblique aura of impropriety because they employed the unnatural voice of the castrato.

Mozart and Verdi have been restored to honored places in the hierarchy. Gluck is admired for his music as well as his historical importance, despite the painful evidence that so far from casting the works of Metastasio and Satan behind him he returned repeatedly to the fleshpots after the success of his first reform operas. More recent, and more remarkable, has been the discovery that the early seventeenth century produced a dramatic composer of the highest genius in Monteverdi. In effect the conventions used by all these composers have become acceptable. This is not the case with Handel, at any rate where the general public is concerned. But we ought to pause before condemning him a priori because he employed an obsolete convention. His operas are period pieces; but so in the true sense are those of Mozart and Verdi and Wagner. The question is, can they transcend their period? Are they worth the initial effort involved in coming to grips with them?

It would be vain to deny the limitations of opera seria; the case for the prosecution must be squarely faced. If we open the score of a Handel opera, or any Italian opera of the period, we are confronted with a long string of arias for solo voice introduced and separated by secco recitative, that is, recitative accompanied only by a bass part, figured or unfigured, which was filled out by the continuo harpsichord player.

The recitative would seem to enshrine the maximum of action in the minimum of music. In the arias the reverse obtains: one character after another holds forth about the situation in which he finds himself and immediately leaves the stage. There are occasional short ariosos, nearly always at the beginning of a scene, that are not followed by an exit; but the vast majority of the arias are in da capo form—a first part in the tonic key, a second part, often on the same thematic material but shorter and in a contrasted key or mode, and a repeat of the first part that is not written out in the score. At rare moments of tension the recitative is accompanied by the orchestra—usually, though not invariably, the strings and continuo. These accompanied recitatives offered the composer his most obvious opportunity to express emotional conflict. For this reason they are the easiest things for a modern audience to accept as genuinely dramatic, especially since the method of treating them changed little throughout the eighteenth century and continued well into the nineteenth.

Duets are introduced sparingly, and for the most part confined to set pieces, also in da capo form, in which a pair of lovers welcome or bewail their destiny. Ensembles for more than two voices are very rare, and most operas have no chorus in the modern sense. The one occasion when the audience could rely on hearing all or most of the voices singing together came at the end of the opera, when a brief concerted piece in dance rhythm and simple block harmony brought down the curtain on a conventional happy end. This is called a coro or chorus, but was sung by the soloists. There is an overture in several movements, with little apparent relation to what follows in the opera, and a few short instrumental pieces here and there to represent such events as battles or ceremonial functions. These too are very simple, often no more than a token flourish or fanfare.

This sort of musical design is of course reflected in the libretto. A system that concentrates action in the recitatives (which were sung in a rapid parlando style) and emotional expression in the arias seems likely to unfold the opera in an alternation of jerks and pauses that scarcely conduces to artistic coherence. The exit convention does not help. Sometimes an aria will arise naturally from the dramatic situation and lead to an exit; but it is no easy matter to design a plot in which this happens twenty or thirty times and almost no other sequence is possible. A character threatening another with violence, murder, or rape cannot get on with the job; he has to leave his potential victim and go out. The librettist then starts building anew. His task is to evolve a sequence of strong aria situations for each character in turn, and they must be sufficiently varied to evoke arias in as many different moods as possible—vengeful, despairing, amorous, reflective, pathetic, and so on. Even if he succeeds in constructing a plot in which the characters behave consistently—and the best Italian librettists achieved a good deal in this direction—the action is bound to appear complicated by the standards of later opera. If he is less successful, it may degenerate into the absurd or the obscure.

The exit convention is not quite invariable, but it is very nearly so. The few Handel operas where it is sometimes ignored, such as *Agrippina, Rinaldo,* and *Serse,* owe their exception to a historical reason.[4] If it is necessary for the departing singer to appear in the next scene we may find the librettist sending him off and at once bringing him back, or perhaps inserting the stage direction *offers to retire.* Another gambit was to let him go to sleep on stage. This seems to have counted as an exit, though it generally followed an arioso and not a full-scale aria. It is remarkable how often Handel's characters fall asleep in view of the audience, and still more remarkable how he makes this license serve his musical and dramatic design.

Often the librettist has to get rid of a character without the drama supplying him with any valid reason to do so. A favorite method of achieving this was the so-called simile aria, an elaborate set piece in which the singer, before departure, compares his situation to that of a steersman adrift in a storm, a turtle-dove waiting for his mate, a Hyrcanian tigress threatened with the loss of her young, or some other phenomenon of natural history involving birds, animals, or changes in the weather. This looks deplorable from the dramatic point of view, since apart from bringing the action to a full stop—or rather a prolonged fermata—it throws the emphasis not on the character's emotional response but on an external parallel that may be forced or superficial.

---

[4] *Agrippina* and *Serse* reflect an older Venetian tradition. *Rinaldo* was an attempt to establish a new tradition suited to English taste.

The historical explanation of the exit and simile arias, and of much else in the opera seria convention, lies of course in the enormous esteem enjoyed by the singers. The da capo aria was the perfect vehicle for vocal virtuosity, since the singer could for the moment forget that he was part of a larger whole and address himself to dazzling the audience, adding embellishments and cadenzas in the second part and especially the da capo (where the listener, having heard the tune straight, could easily appreciate them) and then retire into the wings—pursued, if he was lucky, by applause—and await his next chance to shine. This satisfied the singer and the audience; we should not assume that it annoyed the composer. It is a mistake, in opera or any other art, to write down virtuosity as a defect. This idea is a legacy of Puritanism. The trouble comes with the misuse of virtuosity to express nothing but itself, to create a spiritual vacuum; and this is a sin against art, not against morals. That is not the only defense of the da capo aria. Contemporary theorists pointed out that no passion—and each aria was supposed to express one passion or *Affekt*—can be sustained for long without losing its potency. The second part, however short, gave sufficient contrast for the passion to burst into renewed flame with the da capo.

Anyone who reads the libretto of a Handel opera, especially of the heroic type, without the music and then imagines it sung in the manner described may indeed receive the impression of a spiritual vacuum. Although this derives in part from the fallacy that an opera's dramatic potency can be judged from its libretto alone, we ought to probe further the premises on which it rests. It is true that while the passions of the characters often loom larger than life, they seldom produce conclusive actions—until the end of the opera, when everything falls into place with an all-too-often-unconvincing click. The reason why these warriors constantly threaten each other with daggers but use none, and why they are always throwing each other into dungeons—a fate that overtakes the entire cast in rotation in some operas, like *Giustino* and *Faramondo*—is that these are the quickest methods of producing that succession of sudden shifts of fortune on which the convention depends for its aria situations. If a character is killed, he is of no more use to the plot, since he cannot react to his own death, and there is a limit to the reactions of the others. In an opera with a small cast and no chorus a death may create difficulties of another kind. The bass is usually the villain, and therefore the most subject to casualty; but if he is killed there may be no one left to sing the bass part in the coro. In at least two operas, *Flavio* and *Sosarme*, Handel gets round this by the singular method of making the dead bass sing his part from the wings. The same situation arises with potential suicides: the threat is more serviceable to the librettist than the deed. Hence someone rushes in at the last minute and prevents the dagger from being pushed home. When a character does succeed in committing suicide, like Melissa in *Amadigi* and Bajazet in *Tamerlano*, Handel seizes his chance and writes music of great tragic power.

The same rule of inconclusiveness applies to the lusts of the flesh, producing results that strike us as ludicrous, though that does not often seem to have been the intention. In *Silla* the Roman dictator commits seven indecent assaults on stage in rapid succession, without making any impression on the virtue of the two ladies concerned, and has repeatedly to take refuge in an indignant and undignified exit. Pompey's widow Cornelia in *Giulio Cesare* is the target of improper advances from three of the other characters, which open the way for arias of complaint and vengeance from her and her son Sesto. Needless to say, she escapes unscathed. The only Handel character who does not, Florinda in the early opera *Rodrigo*, has an illegitimate child by a married man, and the child is brought on as a pawn in the plot. But this is exceptional, and the affair is over before the opera begins. It is significant that the few Handel operas in which characters are found living in sin are magic operas like *Alcina*, antiheroic comedies like *Flavio* and *Deidamia*, and the half-realistic, half-romantic *Ariodante*. In the heroic operas more is threatened, but less is performed. This state of affairs may have its distant origin in the seventeenth-century librettist's identification of his characters with members of the princely court for which he was writing, and in his desire to be tactful rather than true to life.[5]

The spiritual climate of opera seria is as remote from Christianity as it is from Freud. In Italy the censorship forbade all mention of God and the Christian religion; and it is curious to note that the libretto of *Rinaldo*, a new piece written for London, though it purports to deal

---

[5] This is not to say that he could not wield a satirical pen; see p. 100 below.

with the capture of Jerusalem during the First Crusade, is so pagan in
spirit that it borrows its imagery and even its minor characters from
Greek and Nordic mythology, making great play with Amazons, Furies, dragons, and mermaids. The cast includes a so-called Christian Magician, who helps the Crusaders to storm Armida's enchanted castle, but
his methods are highly unclerical and have more in common with those
of Zoroastro or even Armida herself than with any Christian activity.

The opera seria libretto takes us into a world of threats and blackmail, in which emotions are unconfined but action is limited. It is an
elaborate game played by artificial rules. But so in a different way is the
dramma giocoso of Da Ponte in *Don Giovanni* and *Così fan tutte*. Handel's plots and characters, like Mozart's, can convey an impression of
psychological subtlety and profundity, often in flashes and sometimes
throughout a whole opera. In both cases this is due to the broad humanity and sympathy of the composer transfiguring the material offered
by the libretto.

The parallel is not exact, for it would be idle to deny that (with
perhaps a few exceptions) the audience of Handel's day showed little
or no interest in opera as continuous drama; had this not been so, the
art would have developed differently. De Brosses, Burney, and other
writers have left ample testimony on this point. In Italy it was usual
for the audience to gossip, eat, drink, talk politics, and play cards in
their boxes, only stopping to listen when one of their favorite singers
came on. In England their behavior may have been a little more orderly,
but probably not much. According to Burney they regarded the arias
of what he called the subaltern or cadet singers as occasions for discussing the merits of their betters. They certainly listened to the stars—Senesino, Cuzzoni, Faustina, and the rest—and made a great noise at the
end of their arias, cheering, countercheering, and arguing about their relative status. Not unnaturally they had little use for quartets, trios, and
duets: how could one judge the soprano if the contralto kept chipping
in? Many of them did not understand Italian and were bored by the recitatives, though the printed librettos on sale in the theater gave a line-by-
line English translation as well as the cast and the argument of the plot.
Burney's own attitude emerges from his habit, when discussing the score
of an opera, of referring to the names of the singers, not of the charac-

ters. But Burney, though he had known Handel in his last years and played in his orchestra during the oratorio period, wrote his *History of Music* more than a generation later. Much as he admired Handel, there is plenty of evidence that he misunderstood his achievement; and he never heard him conduct any of his operas.

It is hardly surprising that composers as well as others saw opera seria in terms of a body of detached and detachable arias. Burney says specifically that they were not expected to waste time or talent on the cadet singers. Even if they possessed a gift for dramatic composition, they had little inducement to put it into practice; they could only do so on any scale by wrestling with the convention, and few of them seem to have had any such ambition. Hence too the vogue of the pasticcio opera. Since similar situations recurred in every libretto, arias were easily interchangeable—from scene to scene, from opera to opera, and from composer to composer. When a new opera was needed in a hurry, the resident composer had only to take an existing libretto, collect two dozen or so arias of his own or someone else's (possibly from several different authors) and link them together with recitative. The audience did not mind inconsistency of style,[6] provided the singers met with their approval. Handel himself put together a few pasticcios from his own work, and some of his revivals of earlier operas come very close to this;[7] but he did not normally allow singers to interpolate arias by other composers. The sole exception, the *Poro* revival of 1736 (when the castrato Annibali, who had just arrived in London and had never sung in a Handel opera, introduced two arias by Ristori and one by Vinci), was probably an emergency measure enforced by Handel's ill health at that period.

All this, needless to say, is repulsive to modern ideas of what an opera—any opera of any age—ought to be. It seems to us to put first things last; the singer above the composer, the aria above the opera, the incident above the plot. Whether we go to Monteverdi or Wagner, Mozart or Verdi, we like the drama to be dissolved in the music, not shut

---

[6] This would in any case be less marked in the eighteenth century than later, especially among minor composers. Opera seria tended to produce a generic idiom, which changed comparatively slowly.

[7] Notably *Tolomeo* in 1730 and *Il Pastor Fido* in May 1734.

off in a series of separate compartments, and we like it to develop in orderly progression from scene to scene, with the dramatic and musical climaxes coinciding at focal points. The opera seria convention would appear to have two almost fatal defects, not to mention many minor ones. Its concentration on the solo voice imposes a monotony of texture likely to sap the composer's invention and put a modern audience to sleep. And the equally exclusive preoccupation with recitative and the da capo aria bids fair to inhibit any structural development over a longer stretch than a single scene. No wonder historians have sat heavily on the opera seria and all its works. No wonder posterity has applauded Gluck's reforms and swept his operatic predecessors one and all under the counter. If this were the whole story, if Handel had not found some method of reconciling the convention with the demands of the drama instead of abdicating to the audience and the singers, there would indeed be no case for reviving his operas today and little point in writing about them.

There remains another group of conventions with which the student of opera seria must come to terms, those that govern the choice and treatment of the principal voices. The most conspicuous and most notorious is the use of the castrato. There are obvious impediments to our acceptance of a class of opera in which the hero, who may be a famous conqueror like Julius Caesar or Alexander the Great or Richard Coeur-de-Lion, and who is always the most ardent of lovers, is sung not by a tenor or even a baritone, but by a castrato. Sometimes the villain of the piece is another castrato—Tamerlano for instance or Tolomeo in *Giulio Cesare;* this may be a little easier to accept, especially for a generation that has heard a countertenor Oberon in Benjamin Britten's *Midsummer Night's Dream.* The practical problems for modern performance are discussed in chapter 11 below. It will suffice here to state the fact and correct the emphasis in two respects that are almost invariably misunderstood.

First, the association in the minds of Handel and his contemporaries was not entirely—perhaps not predominantly—between the lover-hero and the castrato, but between the lover-hero and the high voice, whether soprano or alto. A large number of these male roles were not written for castrati at all, but for women. Handel's operas contain at least twenty-six male roles composed for women, and eight or nine others, first sung by castrati, that he gave to women in revivals. They include heroes, generals, and Roman Emperors.[8] A first-rate castrato was a great public draw, and if he was available he naturally got the best part. A secondary castrato did not. In the original production of *Radamisto*, one of Handel's most important operas and his first contribution to the Royal Academy of Music, the two largest male parts, including the hero, were sung by women, and only the third by a castrato.

Secondly, this use of high voices, far from being less dramatically convincing than modern practice, is often more so. Many opera seria plots depend on a woman disguising herself as a man—the *Fidelio* situation. In Handel's *Siroe*, *Partenope*, *Alcina*, and *Serse* one of the chief characters is so disguised all through, and the situation occurs prominently in other operas, such as *Admeto*. Since the principal agent of the drama was the voice, the similarity of pitch is a dramatic advantage. The popularity of castrato and travesti roles had one side effect that may be less easy to appreciate today; it encouraged a good deal of sexual innuendo and double entendre, not always of the politest nature, in the librettos. On the continent this was complicated by the fact that castrati sometimes played female roles,[9] though this does not appear to have occurred in England. But more than one of Handel's plots revolves round a situation of this type. In *Deidamia* we find a woman playing the part of the hero, the young Achilles, who throughout the opera is disguised as a woman; in which situation he (or she) enjoys a clandestine love affair, with the audience in the know but not the rest of the cast. This species of dramatic irony, as well as the use of a high voice for the hero,[10] persisted long after Handel. It forms the pivot of one of the most amusing of Rossini's early comedies, *L'Equivoco stravagante*, in which the heroine's young lover frightens off an elderly admirer by pretending that she is a castrato in disguise.

The whole vocal structure of opera seria, and consequently the in-

[8] For example, Valentiniano in *Ezio*. The casting did not imply any effeminacy in the character.

[9] Especially in Rome, where for long periods women were excluded from the operatic stage by Papal decree.

[10] In the Shakespeare operas of the early romantic period in Italy, Romeo and Hamlet were regularly played by women.

strumental texture as well, was based on the predominance of high voices. One of Handel's operas, *Amadigi,* has no solo voice below a contralto, and in several others there is only a minor part for low voice. Half of them contain no tenor role; where there is a tenor he never plays the hero, as in romantic opera or the operas of Handel's French contemporaries. He is an old man or a tyrant or a general of mature experience. Basses were similarly restricted. There are a few exceptions; but in the vast majority of operas, not only Handel's but everyone else's, sopranos and altos were associated with youth and innocence, tenors and basses with age and experience. Sometimes the hero is a soprano and the heroine a contralto, so that in a duet the male has the higher part. Of course the casting of every opera depended on the singers available; but the opera seria composer never distributed the voices in the manner we might expect from later practice. Even when Handel had all four types of voice in his company, which happened in the seasons of 1724-1726, 1729-1732, and 1735-1737, he seldom gave the tenor or the bass the prominence we should regard as his due.[11]

[11] The principal exceptions are the tenor parts he wrote for Borosini in *Tamerlano* and *Rodelinda,* and for Fabri in *Lotario* and *Poro.*

CHAPTER 2

🏵🏵🏵🏵🏵🏵🏵🏵🏵🏵🏵

Handel's Solution

It is impossible to assess Handel's response to the challenge of opera seria unless we are prepared to consider his operas as wholes, for all their appearance of a jumble of disconnected parts, and to visualize them as he intended them to be played, sung, and acted. Nothing is easier than to form a false judgment from a cursory reading of the score or from a performance that obscures the composer's aim, whether by insensitive cutting, distorting the texture, or playing ducks and drakes with the plot.

Even if it is printed correctly, the score of an opera seria, one of Handel's in particular, can mislead on several levels. It is an outline in a single dimension, and incomplete at that. If we read it as we read a score of Mozart or Verdi, we may be in for a complete deception. There are at least three reasons for this. The first is surprising: of all the great classical composers, Handel is perhaps the most difficult to judge from the printed page, not because he is complex but because he can be so simple. He had an acute ear for texture, for vocal and instrumental combinations of every kind, and an equally sure sense of when to introduce a period formula—melodic, harmonic, or rhythmic—with the most devastating effect.

Secondly, baroque composers did not write down anything like all they intended to be heard, even such things as trills and appoggiaturas that the singer or player was obliged to perform—much less those on which he was expected to exercise his taste. Few things look more dreary on paper than a page of secco recitative. But it need not sound so, especially if it possesses the strong harmonic and modulatory frame-

work it generally has in Handel. Playing from a bare or figured bass was
a recognized feature of musical education, and a good continuo player,
with the singers acting with the voice and supplying the necessary appoggiaturas, could—and still can—turn the recitative into a taut and
dramatic means of conveying ideas, impulses, and emotions. This is much
more true of the arias. Although the da capo was not written out, it
was never a literal repeat. The variations introduced by the singer and
the continuo player (who was usually the composer), whether planned
in advance or improvised on the spur of the moment, could vary not
only the detail but the whole impact of the da capo. If performers are
to recreate this effect today, they must learn from the beginning by
immersing themselves in the style of the music; this may not be easy, but
it can be done.

Thirdly, of almost equal importance for the opera as a whole is the
scenic element, the tradition of which has been buried by subsequent
developments in the theater. Again it can be largely recovered. There
were many strands in opera seria—concert, pantomime, military tattoo,
ballet, and court masque among them—and although the constituents
varied according to time and place, and not all were necessarily present
together, the visual aspect was never negligible. Many operas, including
a number of Handel's, involved spectacular tableaux and transformations
quite as elaborate as those demanded by Spontini, Meyerbeer, Wagner,
and even Schoenberg in *Moses and Aaron*.[1] This made for a great deal
of variety; and, paradoxical as it may sound, variety and not monotony
is the most striking feature of Handel's finest operas. In order to understand what opera seria was aiming at we must think of it as a kind of
Gesamtkunstwerk. The librettos are more than a verbal scaffold for the
composer; the music is only one element, albeit the most important.

When we look further into the plan and execution of the operas,
one fact becomes increasingly clear. Handel's entire approach, from
the choice of tonality that sometimes governs whole operas down to
the innumerable modifications of da capo form, stems from a coherent
conception of opera as drama.[2] This is true even when a faulty libretto

---

[1] See pp. 77–80 and 131–133 below.

[2] His method of composition is significant in this connection. Unlike many
opera composers, he worked straight through the libretto, an act at a time, settling

appears to inhibit any sort of unity. We may wonder why he ever accepted some librettos, or if he had much choice in the matter; no one knows the answer. He was often defeated; but much more remarkable are his successes against odds, the occasions when he neutralizes or turns to advantage the limitations of the convention and the defects of a particular libretto. Sometimes he can administer a correction while the opera is on its course with a skill as seemingly miraculous as that of a scientist diverting a missile aimed at the moon.

Handel was not only a great composer; he was a dramatic genius of the first order born in an unfavorable age, a period whose operatic convention was as near as possible antidramatic. In a sense his whole career was a struggle against rebarbative material and conditions, an attempt to make bricks with a minimum of straw and to build those bricks into durable architecture. It is the mark of supreme genius, in the arts as elsewhere, to bring off triumphantly just those things that the rest of mankind considers impossible. Could anyone have imagined a cohesive drama lasting for four evenings if Wagner had not written *The Ring?* We too easily assume, from the disjointed appearance of opera seria and the behavior of its audiences, that it was impossible for a great artist to impose a unifying stamp on it, regardless of whether the contemporary listener was likely or even able to grasp the full implications of such an achievement. That after all is more or less what Handel did with the dramatic oratorio. It is possible that this brilliant synthesis, in which he overcame the prohibition of stage performance and a progressive misunderstanding of his aims by composing for a theater of the imagination, would never have been achieved had he not for years been engaged in a similar struggle in the opera house, trying to reconcile dramatic movement with a static convention. Opera seria was a veritable bow of Odysseus; but in the end Odysseus came along and drew it. Unlike the summary proceedings of Alexander with the Gordian knot, Handel's was a creative achievement.

His solution was characteristic of himself and his age. While from time to time and for special purposes he introduced many formal, textural, and technical variants into his operas, which are consequently less

---

the framework of the arias and inserting the recitatives later. Thus the tonal scheme was established at the start.

uniform than those of his contemporaries, the main field for the activity of his genius remained the confines of the opera seria convention. He asserted his mastery not by abrogating the convention but by working within it—stretching its bounds on occasion, but never breaking them. This was the method of nearly all the great composers of the eighteenth century, Bach and Mozart in particular. Like them Handel not only accepted the current conventions; he found his inspiration in them. Whatever he may have done later in oratorio, in his operas he rejoiced in the da capo aria, the high voice, and the virtuoso singer, even in the exit aria and the happy end—not because they made his task easier, but because they gave him a framework he could modify, a mean from which he could profitably deviate and to which he could all the more profitably return.

The point here is an axiom of aesthetics. The more restricted a convention within which an artist works, the greater the scope for achieving the maximum effect with the minimum means, always provided he has the stature to command his materials. One of the most potent weapons in the armory of any composer is the ability, with the help of a formula or convention, to lead his audience to expect one thing and then surprise them by doing something different. Many of the supreme strokes in the music of the Viennese symphonists depend on their use of the sonata principle in this way. A familiar instance is the passage of suspense before the recapitulation in the first movement of the Eroica Symphony, where one of the horns anticipates the return of the tonic while the rest of the orchestra is still holding the dominant harmony. This would be as nonsensical as Beethoven's publisher thought when he tried to "correct" it, but for the fact that the audience, consciously or not, knows what to expect and is waiting for the tonic. Beethoven exploits their knowledge and catches them on the wrong foot. The restrictions of a closed or partially closed form become, in the hands of a master, the gateway to freedom.

Just as Beethoven or Haydn or Mozart uses sonata form to arouse, prolong, or disappoint expectation, Handel uses the da capo aria and the other opera seria conventions. Any performance that tends to weaken these links treats Handel as Hercules treated Antaeus: by lifting him from the element in which he worked, it deprives him of one of his main sources of strength, the skill with which he reconciled his native dramatic genius with the conditions imposed by contemporary taste. This is not just an intellectual feat; it is the very kernel of his art. Unless the modern conductor and stage director keep a firm grasp of these conditions, they cannot get inside the convention or interpret it to the audience; and unless the audience grows sufficiently familiar with the convention to sense, however unconsciously, any deviation from it, it cannot comprehend the measure of Handel's genius or receive his operas as works of art. It may take a point here and there, savor a modulation or enjoy a melody; but it will miss far more. This, not mere pedantry, is the principal reason for demanding authenticity in performance. As Ellen Terry once remarked, you cannot be eccentric unless you know where the circle is. The conductor who tries too hard to temper the opera to the shorn lamb has only himself to blame if the lamb shivers and goes home before the end.

All great opera composers have certain gifts in common, apart from a sufficiency of purely musical invention: the power to draw character in music (and character that develops in the course of the action), to project incident with peculiar vividness, to control a large-scale design by means of formal or tonal balances, and to reconcile the claims of variety and unity. But the opera seria composer confronts a form with a strong centrifugal tendency: to hold it together he needs exceptional powers of organization and perhaps an extra ration of musical invention. Otherwise it disintegrates. If he is to get the awkward contrivance off the ground in one piece, he cannot afford to relax his standards of structural stability. He must consider each aria's place in the design, even—indeed especially—when he is humoring the subaltern singers. In fact he needs to think in terms not of the aria but of the act and the whole opera, and on another level (since an aria can express only a single mood or at best a conflict of two moods) in terms of the entire part of each character.

That Handel possessed these powers has been demonstrated in a few—a very few—modern stage productions. In the theater, under a conductor and director who understand them, the best of his operas can make a very powerful impact, far stronger than that of the contemporary operas of Rameau with their superficially more varied structure and means of expression. The reason is that while Rameau's forms are essentially a series of miniatures expanded to the scale desired, Handel from the start adjusts his thinking to the span of his subject.[3] In these operas (*Tamerlano*, *Orlando*, and *Alcina* are examples) the music is not only on the highest level throughout; it is almost all indispensable. It becomes difficult to cut anything without detracting from a unity that appears to have little or no basis in the written notes. Many of the operas fall below this standard (it does not follow that they are never worth hearing); this is to be expected, since such a narrowly based form allows little margin for error. But when Handel could identify himself with the plot, and especially when the librettist laid it out in a manner combining human sympathy with dramatic conviction, his imagination was strong enough to reconcile the contrary forces of artistic unity and a centrifugal convention, and (by harnessing the friction between them) to bring off effects unattainable in any other medium.

There are of course occasions when he has to conceal the cracks by sleight of hand. His treatment of simile arias shows him on guard against the potential weakness. He consistently brings his great gifts of musical invention and picturesque evocation to plug the hole in the drama. Many, perhaps most, of these pieces are of such superb quality that only an operatic masochist would dream of cutting them. There are countless examples—Caesar's hunting aria with horn obbligato in *Giulio Cesare* (originally composed for another character), the aria in *Flavio* in which Guido compares himself to an ermine that dislikes getting its fur dirty, or that in *Admeto* where Antigona likens herself to a "coasting sparrow-hawk." The action may pause, as it does for a set piece in operas of all periods, but the music holds us in its grip like the Ancient Mariner. In performance these simile arias are not felt as a weakness nearly so frequently as Dent and others have implied, or as a reading of the libretto might lead us to expect.

Sometimes Handel goes one better by making the music illuminate the character as well as, or in preference to, the simile. In Act III of *Alcina* Ruggiero, reunited with his wife but reluctant to leave her in danger, compares his predicament with that of a tigress unable to abandon her young to the hunters. Strictly the aria "Stà nell'Ircana" should express

---

[3] See for example pp. 140–146 below.

mental conflict or hesitation. But it is dramatically necessary that Ruggiero, who has long been subject to Alcina's sorcery and is about to destroy it, should at least once stand out as a hero, and this is his last aria in the opera. So Handel gives him a splendidly resolute, extroverted piece, free from conflict or hesitation, thereby fulfilling the drama but controverting the simile. And he underlines the point by adding brilliant parts for two horns in G (instead of the more usual F), their first and only appearance in the opera.

Handel did not subscribe to Burney's condescending view of his obligations to the cadet singers. A glance at almost any of his operas shows that, if the character made any appeal to his imagination (and very few did not at some point in the story), he lavished as much care and genius on the inferior singers as on the principals. *Tamerlano*, for example, has a cast of six, of whom the fifth in importance, Irene, was sung by the minor contralto Anna Dotti. In the second act she is rejected by Tamerlano, to whom she is betrothed, but retains a dawning hope that she scarcely dares trust. Her aria "Par che mi nasca" is a miracle of beauty and psychological insight. And Handel wasted plenty of time and talent on it. He had composed it for a soprano who did not appear; instead of simply transposing it for Dotti he expanded and altered it and enriched the scoring, adapting the original flute parts for two cornetti.

A Handel opera is a far more complex and subtly organized phenomenon than it looks on paper. If these operas, including their librettos, are subjected to the detailed scrutiny they deserve but have seldom if ever received, it may be found that Handel's mastery of opera as a fusion of music and drama is scarcely less absolute than that of Monteverdi and Mozart, though it is very differently exercised. And he left enough masterpieces to bridge the hiatus in operatic history between the daring flights of Monteverdi's old age and the beginnings of musical drama as we know it in Gluck and Mozart.

There are links of sympathy and approach between Handel and those three composers that are not perhaps wholly fortuitous. Handel cannot have known Monteverdi's operas, but he was stimulated by the Venetian tradition that inspired and long survived them, as we can see from the libretto and music of his Venice opera *Agrippina*. His influence

on Gluck, with whom he was in contact for a year in London, is more
important than historians allow; it is difficult to believe that certain passages in *Admeto*, *Orlando*, and *Hercules* did not haunt Gluck's memory.
The link with Mozart is the most fascinating of all, since it appears to be
an affinity of genius, though the possibility of influence cannot be ruled
out. The music of no other dramatic composer comes closer to Mozart
in its detached but penetrating insight into human nature, its capacity
to make a profound statement in a frivolous or comic situation, and its
peculiar mixture of irony and pathos, solemnity and grace, tragedy and
serenity. These things can be found from time to time in Handel's
oratorios; in the operas, where he is concerned not with nations or
spiritual concepts but with the emotions and sufferings of individuals,
they are his central preoccupation.

CHAPTER 3

Handel's Operatic Career

Handel's operatic career lasted from 1704 to 1741, nearly twice as long as his oratorio career. During that period he wrote more than forty operas, of which thirty-nine survive, some of them in several versions. Although his style naturally developed, and although certain features were more prominent at some periods than others, there was no radical change in his attitude to opera as an art, or in his choice of subjects. Indeed he seems to frustrate chronological inquiry by doubling back on his tracks and returning to operatic themes and types that had occupied him perhaps much earlier, just as at the end of his life he refashioned musical ideas conceived fifty years before.

From the day when at the age of eighteen he abandoned the organ loft of the cathedral at Halle for the rough and tumble of the Hamburg opera house, Handel spent almost his entire creative life in the theater, the greater part of it struggling with the recalcitrant form of opera seria. It was in opera that he chose to stake his claim for recognition and to make his living, first in Hamburg, then in Italy, then for a full thirty years (with one or two short breaks) in London. Everything in his career was governed by this choice. His church music is relatively unimportant. His chamber cantatas, more than a hundred in number and nearly all written in Italy when opera in the Roman states was under a Papal ban, are operatic scenes in embryo—and sometimes more than embryo. No sharp distinction of form or style can be drawn between them, or his two Italian oratorios, and the operas. He seems to have used the cantata with conscious intent as a training ground in dramatic expression, often of a concentrated and impassioned nature; a good many cantata arias were lifted bodily into his later operas,[1] and still more were drawn on for thematic material. The oratorios of his last years are likewise an extension and fulfillment of his dramatic genius, after the English public had rejected the operas. That he continued to compose operas, nearly all of them failures, for more than eight years after the public had demonstrated its preference for oratorio, is clear proof of devotion to his first love.

Handel wrote several operas for Hamburg, but only the first, *Almira*, survives. This is an immature work in a very mixed style; it is interesting for its revelation of Handel's early environment, but it reflects a local tradition that had no firm roots and whose chief exponent was the similarly eclectic Reinhard Keiser. A public opera house had been established at Hamburg in 1678 in an attempt to naturalize the art in Germany. This was not a court but a free city and a great trading center, and in happier circumstances might have nourished a German school patronized by the middle classes. By Handel's time, however, the local element had been largely ousted by the Italian, as a fruit tree reverts to the stock on which it has been grafted. Hence the polyglot libretto of *Almira*: the arias are sometimes in German, sometimes in Italian; the dialogue and stage directions are sprinkled with French words; a German recitative often introduces an Italian aria. The audience can have had no interest in the literary or dramatic aspects. The plot, borrowed from Italy but only half assimilated, is a maze of obscure and unmotivated intrigue; the mature Handel could scarcely have made it convincing. This confusion was typical of the Hamburg opera, which not surprisingly collapsed a generation later in 1738.

The two operas Handel composed in Italy—there would doubtless have been others but for the Papal ban—are more important, especially the second of them, *Agrippina*. (No one knows when, where, or even if *Rodrigo* was performed.) It was written for one of the public theaters in Venice and was an immediate success. Handel was never again to write an opera for such a sophisticated audience, or for one hearing its own

---

[1] For example the cantata "Crudel tiranno amor" was cannibalized for the first (1722) revival of *Floridante*, in which all three of its arias came to rest, with some alterations to the words.

language. The Venetians, with an operatic tradition going back eighty years, had certain standards in regard to librettos; they were little interested in spectacle, in which a commercial house was at a disadvantage compared with a court,[2] but they liked the heroic element to be spiced with irony, if not with humor. The parallels between *Agrippina* and Monteverdi's *Coronation of Poppea* are not confined to the presence of some of the same characters, or to the fascinating and unexplored affinities between the dramatic approach of the two composers. There is a similar flavor in the librettos, which take historical figures and cut them abruptly down to size, though Monteverdi's has a supernatural element absent from Handel's. The important thing is that Venetian taste left a permanent mark on Handel; it can be traced all through his London operas, especially when he was setting an old Venetian text. And it is interesting to find that many librettos not originally written for Venice —*Partenope, Ariodante, Arminio,* and *Berenice* among them—reached him through an intermediate Venetian adaptation.

His thirty-six remaining operas were composed for London; one, the unimportant *Silla,* for private performance at Burlington House,[3] the rest for one or other of the public theaters. Although he held an appointment at the English court, and his operatic activities were to some extent patronized by the royal family, his position was not that of a continental *Kapellmeister,* who was required to satisfy the musical demands of his ruler. Handel's career was not typical of his age. As an operatic center London had something in common with Hamburg. A shallow-rooted vernacular opera was being undermined by the Italian opera seria, which had been introduced a few years before Handel's arrival late in 1710. Most of these early Italian imports were pasticcios, and some, as at Hamburg, were polyglot entertainments sung in a mixture of Italian and English. The new style, despite (or because of) its lack of local associations, was all the rage with the aristocracy. Thus there was no tradition, such as there had been at Venice, on which Handel could build, and he had no security of tenure. He was a free

[2] With the possible exception of *Rodrigo,* Handel never composed an opera for a court.

[3] On June 2, 1713. The only known copy of the libretto is in the Huntington Library, San Marino, California.

lance, who had to win and hold the attention of his audience. His position remained essentially unaltered for the next thirty years. When public taste changed, Handel had to make adjustments. This explains most of the developments perceptible in his later operas. Eventually the rival attractions of ballad opera and oratorio took away his audience; but it is a remarkable tribute to his powers that he held their interest, writing in an alien form and a foreign language, for as long as he did.

Handel's London operas can be divided into five periods. The first, from 1711 to 1715, included five works, of which the earliest, *Rinaldo*, though by no means the best, was the most successful and influential. This was the first Italian opera composed specifically for London; and although it is not easy to appreciate the fact today, it was a conscious attempt to establish a local variety of opera seria. The moving spirit was the manager of the Haymarket Theatre, Aaron Hill, who sketched the libretto in English and gave it to Giacomo Rossi to translate into Italian. Hill had his own ideas about opera as an art form and twenty years later in a famous letter[4] did his best to convert Handel to opera in English. In his dedication and preface to the printed libretto of *Rinaldo*, he proclaimed his "Endeavour, to see the English Opera more splendid than her Mother, the Italian," and remarked of the Italian operas hitherto produced in London "that wanting the Machines and Decorations, which bestow so great a Beauty on their Appearance, they have been heard and seen to very considerable Disadvantage." Hill's resolve to spare no expense in satisfying eye and ear resulted in a kind of pantomime, half Italian opera and half Purcellian masque. (It is worth noting that had Purcell survived he would have been no older than 52, an age at which Handel was still writing operas.)

Hill included something for everyone, not forgetting the groundlings. They may have been only spiritual groundlings (the English aristocracy, then as now, was not conspicuous for exalted taste), but the appeal was directed as widely as possible to lovers of singing, spectacle, theatrical machinery, magic, dancing, military maneuvers, and a good stage scrap. Canary-fanciers fared particularly well, since in addition to a large cast of Italian singers, including three castrati, the ritornello

---

[4] Otto Erich Deutsch, *Handel, a Documentary Biography* (London, 1955), p. 299.

of Almirena's aria "Augelletti che cantate" was accompanied by the release of a flock of live birds, which left their mark not only on the opera and the press, in the persons of Addison and Steele, but on the heads of the audience. Another of Hill's innovations was a tentative move away from the exit aria; but he lacked the skill to make much use of this liberty.

As a work of art *Rinaldo* cannot be called a success. Hill emphasized the spectacular element, which is fantastically elaborate,[5] at the expense of the development of character, and Handel had neither the experience nor perhaps the inclination to make good the defect. He hastily adapted a great deal of music from works composed in Italy[6] (hence Rossi's complaint that Handel scarcely gave him time to write the libretto), and although much of it is strikingly beautiful, it remains a hotchpotch. Nevertheless it established Handel's position in London, and it probably confirmed the audience's enthusiasm for the superficialities of the Italian style, its ease, brilliance, and clarity, the sharp contrast between recitative and aria (an aid for the lazy listener), and the virtuosity of the singers. Furthermore it saddled London's commercial theater with the extravagant trappings of continental court opera (including the greatest singers in the market), and hence with a financial drain that was to produce chronic embarrassment in future years. The castrati caused a certain lifting of eyebrows and shrugging of shoulders, and in some quarters open hostility, but they were a source of wonder and astonishment and were soon pursued by fashionable ladies with extravagant hopes. There was so much to enjoy in *Rinaldo* that few people bothered about the weak handling of the drama.

Of the next four operas, two—*Teseo* and *Amadigi*—continued to exploit the magic and spectacular veins, with greater maturity in the music. But it is doubtful if Handel's heart was ever in Hill's ideas for establishing an English variant of opera seria, if indeed they were practicable. He was not to know that the rest of his life was to be spent in London. He wrote no new operas between 1715 and 1720, when the

---

[5] See pp. 77–79 below.

[6] Nearly two-thirds of the vocal movements, other than recitatives, are based in whole or part on earlier music. Some of them, like Argante's first aria (borrowed from Polifemo in *Aci, Galatea e Polifemo*), have scant relevance to their context.

form fell temporarily out of favor, but continued his dramatic career with the two Cannons masques, *Acis and Galatea* and the first *Esther*, destined to become the seed of the English oratorio.

His most fertile period as an opera composer began in 1720 with the foundation of the Royal Academy of Music under the patronage of George I and the nobility. This was a society designed to maintain regular seasons of Italian opera at the King's Theatre in the Haymarket. Handel was given a post as composer, with Giovanni Bononcini and later Attilio Ariosti as his colleagues, and took steps to assemble a company of the leading singers in Europe. His first opera for the Royal Academy, *Radamisto*, is a landmark. It was by far the finest opera seria hitherto heard in London; it employed the largest orchestra, including horns (their operatic début in England) as well as trumpets; and it shows Handel's absolute mastery of the form for the first time.

During the eight years of the Royal Academy, before subscriptions were exhausted and acrimony broke out on and off stage, the King's Theatre came nearest to the continental type of court opera. This is reflected in the librettos, which (with one exception) belong to the heroic-dynastic type in which historians have seen an attempt to glorify the monarch and the ruling social order. Too much can be made of this in connection with Handel, who was no mere court hanger-on. One of his fourteen Academy operas, *Riccardo Primo*, does identify its hero with George II; but this was the result of a last-minute change of plan, and it was intended to celebrate not only the new monarch's coronation but Handel's naturalization as an Englishman. It was in large part a tribute to the nation that had received him permanently into its ranks. On the other hand another libretto of this period, *Flavio*—the exception noted above—has an element of parody so delicate that this masterpiece of tragicomedy has been constantly mistaken for a heroic opera that went wrong; and although easy to produce and requiring nothing in the way of spectacle, it was never revived between 1732 and 1967. The disappearance of the magic element from the Academy operas is significant, but there were still many spectacular scenes of a military and ceremonial nature.

At the Royal Academy Handel was writing for the foremost singers of his age, a fact that certainly contributed to the superb quality of most of these operas. Like other great opera composers he found direct inspiration in both the vocal and instrumental material at his disposal. This was the period of Senesino's first ascendancy and of the great sopranos Cuzzoni and Faustina, whose rivalry ended by straining Handel's muse as well as his temper and bringing the Academy into public ridicule just when the popularity of *The Beggar's Opera* established a rival attraction. For one season Handel enjoyed the rare services of a first-rate tenor in Borosini, who figured prominently in two of his best operas, *Tamerlano* and *Rodelinda*. Together with the preceding work, *Giulio Cesare*, these represent one of the peaks of his career. The falling-off in quality of the later Academy operas, which is a matter of dramatic unity rather than musical invention, was almost certainly due to the presence of two jealous prima donnas each anxious to outshine the other. In order to prepare the lists for this contest, the libretto had to be manipulated so that the two parts had equal prominence, vocally if not dramatically. It may be evidence of Handel's tact that he wrote only one duet for Cuzzoni and Faustina, a short piece in *Alessandro*, the first opera in which they sang together, just as in his whole career he composed a single duet for two castrati. This was in *Tamerlano*; and he cut it before performance. These animals were too dangerous to be put in the same cage.

The failure of the Royal Academy was followed by a blank season, during which Handel visited the continent to collect fresh singers and strengthen his acquaintance with the contemporary Neapolitan style of composers like Vinci and Pergolesi, traces of which can be found in his later operas. It would not have been new to him; some operas of this school had been heard in London, notably *Elpidia*, a pasticcio from Vinci and Orlandini, produced with considerable success at the King's Theatre in May 1725. After his continental tour came the four years of the so-called Second Academy (1729–1733), when Handel was in partnership with the impresario Heidegger, still at the King's Theatre, and composed six new operas. The first, *Lotario*, is a throwback to the Academy manner, with a heavy dynastic libretto and big virtuoso arias. The second, *Partenope*, is an ironic comedy that holds up the stock figures and situations of heroic opera to merciless ridicule. The fact that it is written in a much lighter style, with shorter arias and more ensembles and or-

chestral movements, may just possibly be connected with the success of
the new ballad operas. But it is more likely to reflect Handel's response
to a different type of libretto. For these two operas, *Lotario* and *Partenope*, were written for the same cast of singers. We find a parallel situation much later, in 1748, when Handel composed the most massive of
his oratorios, *Solomon*, with its double choruses and huge orchestra, and
the most delicate and light-hearted, *Susanna*, for the same company in
the same season.

The other four operas of the Second Academy, *Poro*, *Ezio*, *Sosarme*, and *Orlando*, show a very high level of musical invention, and
Orlando is a masterpiece by any standard. It is also Handel's first magic
opera since *Amadigi* eighteen years earlier. But while this naturally involved the use of machines and transformation scenes, the spectacle is
more subordinated to the music than in the first London period. The
characters are far more powerfully realized than those of *Rinaldo*. It is
noteworthy that when Handel revived *Rinaldo* for the last time in
1731, less than two years before *Orlando*, the libretto and the music
were extensively altered. He toned down the extravagances, omitting
(among other things) the fire-spitting dragons and the mermaids, and
gave the opera a new and more convincing end. Armida and her pagan
lover, instead of undergoing an absurd last-minute conversion to Christianity, descend to hell in a chariot, like Medea. Handel may have had
fewer machines and scenic resources; but in all the operas of this period
he concentrates on the inner motives of the characters rather than on
externals. There are also important modifications to the design, in
particular a tendency to build up the coro at the end into a substantial
finale and link it thematically with the preceding movements.[7]

During his fourth London period, from 1734 to June 1737, Handel
was in cut-throat competition with a rival company, the Opera of the
Nobility, which after drawing off some of his best singers, including
Senesino and the bass Montagnana, imported a distinguished composer
in Porpora and the most famous castrato of the eighteenth century,
Farinelli. Handel was temporarily outgunned; apart from the soprano
Anna Strada, few of his singers stayed longer than a year or two, though
some of them, notably the castrati Carestini, Conti, Annibali, and later

[7] See pp. 148–149 below.

Caffarelli, were artists of great ability. The result was a policy of make-shift. After the production of *Arianna* early in 1734 Heidegger let the King's Theatre to the Opera of the Nobility and forced Handel to move to Rich's new theater at Covent Garden. This had the happiest consequences, for Rich had engaged a ballet company with the French dancer Marie Sallé as prima ballerina and choreographer, and a small chorus was available. Handel made full use of these resources in two of his most remarkable operas, *Ariodante* and *Alcina*. The autograph of *Ariodante* furnishes proof that he knew nothing about the move to Covent Garden or the availability of the ballet till almost the last moment, after he had composed the first two acts for a different company of singers. By expelling Handel from the King's Theatre into the arms of Rich the Opera of the Nobility, all unwittingly, made its most signal contribution to history.

Unfortunately Sallé left after one season. Apart from *Atalanta*, an occasional piece of great freshness and charm written to celebrate the wedding of the Prince of Wales, Handel's other Covent Garden operas are disappointing. They contain flashes of genius but a good deal of empty music. One reason for this was undoubtedly ill-health, which prevented him from surmounting a series of weak librettos of the old heroic type.[8] It culminated in a stroke early in 1737. This was followed by the financial collapse both of the Opera of the Nobility and of Handel's enterprise at Covent Garden. When London had failed to support one opera company, it was a curious piece of economics to expect it to patronize two.

Nevertheless the very next season, after a rapid cure at Aachen, Handel was again composing operas, first on commission from Heidegger and later under his own management. This fifth and final period, which ended early in 1741, yielded four new operas, besides a number of pasticcios, odes, and oratorios. All four were failures. The first, *Faramondo*, another throwback, has a complex heroic libretto so cut down, to avoid inflicting too much recitative on the audience, as to be almost incomprehensible. The last three are comedies; although they preserve most of the outward forms of opera seria, and their stories are

---

[8] *Giustino*, which contains an element of pantomime (see p. 173), is a partial exception; but only two or three of the characters come to life.

drawn from ancient history and legend, their spirit is a long way from
the heroic operas of the Royal Academy and from the magic operas.
There is a certain aptness in the fact that Handel, like Verdi, paid his
operatic farewell to the muse of comedy.

During the last two periods his audience and his performers were
changing. The aristocracy, if they were not tiring of Italian opera,
were less willing to support it with their purses. The somewhat more
prominent role that Handel gave to choral and purely orchestral movements in his last operas may have been designed, like the organ concertos in his contemporary oratorios, to appeal to a middle class less
interested in the voice for its own sake. It also reflected the disappearance of the international singers, whom London could no longer afford
to pay. There were still bravura arias, especially for the castrati; but
the operas after *Alcina* (1735) lack the old integration of spectacle,
vocal brilliance, and dramatic expression, and the final comedies depend
not at all on spectacle and very little on vocal display. The singers of
this period, apart from the castrati, were not stars, and many of them
were not Italian; they were English, and largely trained by Handel
himself. The tenor Beard had parts in six new operas and several revivals. Cecilia Young sang in *Ariodante* and *Alcina,* and to judge from
her part in the latter she was a high soprano of no mean order. Others
who appeared were the versatile William Savage,[9] Miss Edwards in the
last two operas, and the Anglo-German basses Waltz and Reinhold.
Imeneo had one Italian in a cast of five, though Francesina, the prima
donna, had been trained in Italy. She was to achieve her greatest triumph in *Semele;* indeed all these singers came to be associated more
with oratorio than with opera.

It has been suggested that Handel's operatic style was out of date.
In a sense this is true, and had been true for a long time; but it is not
a consideration likely to have bothered an English audience, and the
novelty of the oratorios owed nothing to the latest idiom from the continent. What was changing was the taste of the public, which demanded
something more solid and something in its own language. Handel at
last heeded the signs and abandoned opera for ever.

[9] See p. 206 below.

His operatic style was always more flexible than that of his contemporaries, for it could embrace the new without discarding the old. As late as 1738 he was breathing life into the ancient Venetian manner in *Serse*. This eclecticism was a source of strength, not of weakness. His retention of unfashionable polyphonic textures and obsolescent dance rhythms like the Siciliano enriched and varied the music; it did not exclude the means of expression offered by the sparkling if contrapuntally impoverished idiom of the younger Neapolitans. Handel was at once behind and in advance of his age: behind because his natural conservatism refused to surrender what had proved fertile in the past, and perhaps because London lay outside the main stream of opera seria; in advance thanks to the thrust of his genius, which drove him into bold experiments at the demand of the dramatic context. This dualism was to persist throughout the period of the oratorios.

CHAPTER 4

✤✤✤✤✤✤✤✤✤✤✤

The Libretto

Like every dramatic composer, Handel was dependent on the quality of his texts. A composer can make a surprising amount of an unpromising libretto, but he cannot transcend a broken-backed design, in which the behavior of the characters is contradictory and the plot inconsequent or incomprehensible. The man who pays too little attention to such matters, like Schubert, may write wonderful music, but he is not performed. Handel's librettos are commonly held to be outmoded, ridiculous, trivial, obscure, and antidramatic. Outmoded in a historical sense they are, and some deserve the other epithets. But the traditional view of them as a haphazard string of arias and recitatives arranged in no organic sequence is a very long way from the truth. Even if audiences may have regarded them in this light, Handel emphatically and demonstrably did not.

The way to understand his operas is to begin by taking the librettos seriously. Not till then can we make the crucial distinction between apparent absurdities that spring from an unfamiliar convention and genuine absurdities due to an incompetent librettist misusing that convention. It should be no more difficult to reconcile ourselves to the former—to such things as the da capo and the exit aria—than to a dragon singing in *Siegfried* or a crowd of people declaiming eight different things simultaneously in the finale of Act III of *Otello*, provided the music is good enough and librettist and composer employ the convention to some dramatic purpose. The libretto must make sense on its own terms, not on those of another period.

A first glance at Handel's librettos reveals one unpromising fact, which may have helped to discourage enquiry. Very few of them were specifically written for him in the way that Busenello, Calzabigi, Da Ponte, and Boito wrote fresh texts for Monteverdi, Gluck, Mozart, and Verdi. His only new librettos in that sense appear to be those of *Agrippina* and *Rinaldo*, both early works. The others were adaptations of older pieces written for other composers, mostly in Italy.[1] Some of them had passed through several versions and been remodeled successively for three or four composers in as many operatic centers. Moreover, their origins were highly miscellaneous, dating from every decade between the 1650s and the 1730s. The London librettists who sometimes signed the printed texts or their dedications—Rossi, Rolli, and Haym—were no more than hacks. They were attached to the King's Theatre not to supply new works but to refurbish old ones to meet local conditions, including the company of singers available and the tastes of the composer.

This practice, common in the eighteenth century, suggests two lines of enquiry: the origin and previous history of the texts, and the exact nature of the alterations made for Handel. Neither line has been adequately explored, and neither can be followed to its conclusion here, though both would yield valuable evidence. The prehistory is important, since traces of an earlier or a localized tradition survive in some of Handel's librettos and modify to a considerable degree the plan and texture of the music. One consequence of this unrecognized fact has been to lead modern scholars, editors, and performers seriously astray, especially when (as happens with disturbing frequency) the accepted statements or conjectures about the source of a libretto are found to be wrong. For example, the five-act libretto of *Teseo*, for long a puzzle and conjecturally ascribed by Dent to one of Scarlatti's Venetian collaborators, has recently been identified as an adaptation of Quinault's libretto for Lully.[2] The process of modifying a French libretto built round a prominent chorus and ballet for an Italian company employing

[1] In a few instances the original has not been identified.
[2] By J. Merrill Knapp (William C. Smith, *Handel, A Descriptive Catalogue of Early Editions*, London, 1960, p. 76). See also David Kimbell, "The Libretto of Handel's 'Teseo,'" *Music and Letters* (Oct. 1963).

neither and relying entirely on the solo voice explains much that is peculiar in the design of Handel's opera. The same is true of his next opera for the King's Theatre, *Amadigi,* the source of which is Houdar de la Motte's *Amadis de Grèce,* set by Destouches in 1699. Here the original five acts were contracted to three and the choruses eliminated, though a small residue of the ballet survives in Handel's stage directions; its music except for one movement is lost.

There is an even more striking example in the late opera *Serse* of 1738. This has been claimed, rather loosely, as Handel's only comic opera, and its relaxed form—with comparatively few da capo arias (about half the total), much shading of arioso into recitative, and rapid alternation of mood between tragedy, comedy, parody, irony, and farce —has led Rudolf Steglich in the preface to the new Halle score to hail *Serse* as an important step in the development from heroic baroque opera to the *dramma giocoso* of Mozart, under the influence of the Enlightenment and the opera buffa. It is nothing of the sort. The libretto was written for Cavalli in 1654, remodelled by Silvio Stampiglia for Giovanni Bononcini in 1694 (the first opera of a composer who thirty years later was to be Handel's rival in London), and slightly altered for Handel. Stampiglia increased the proportion of exit arias to suit the growing stature of the singer, but the mixed heroic-comic plot and the flexibility of design so unusual in the age of the da capo is a feature of all three versions. Handel was drawing directly on the old Venetian tradition, most familiar today in Monteverdi's *Coronation of Poppea,* which is only a few years earlier than Cavalli's *Serse.* What is more, he borrowed liberally from Bononcini's forty-four-year-old score, expanding and improving the material in his idiosyncratic manner. Every one of the passages that Steglich singles out as advanced for its date happens to be firmly rooted, words and music, in the seventeenth century.[3] *Serse* is not a pre-Viennese but a post-Venetian opera, with its origins in the remote past, long before the rise of the heroic baroque. This does not affect its quality, for it is so deeply impregnated with Handel's genius that it transcends its period. And there is, as will appear, a link with Mozart, though of a different kind.[4]

[3] See the two articles by Harold S. Powers in the *Musical Quarterly* already cited, especially the second (Jan. 1962, pp. 73–92).

[4] See pp. 120–121 below.

The libretto changes made in London were of more than one type, but to judge from the example of *Serse* their chief aim does not seem to have been to bring the text up to date. It is, however, unlikely that such an old plan would have been retained, or this libretto chosen in the first place, if Handel had still been writing for a team of great singers like that of the Royal Academy. Many of the London changes can be traced to the number and quality of the singers available. Women could be cast as heroes and even as villains (such as Polinesso in *Ariodante* and Amanzio in *Giustino*, the one character in a Handel opera whose misdeeds bring him to the scaffold), but a poor singer would not be given a big part. If there were not enough capable artists, one or more parts would be reduced to recitative or cut altogether. In his libretto of *Poro* Metastasio gave Alexander's general Timagene three arias (he is quite an important agent in the plot), but he has none at all in Handel's original (1731) score, because the bass Commano was an inferior singer. The same thing happened in *Siroe*, where another general, Arasse, was sung by another weak bass, Palmerini, and was duly deprived of his three arias. When Handel revived *Poro* after an interval of nine months with Montagnana as Timagene, he did give him three arias; they are, however, not settings of Metastasio, but borrowings from earlier operas. The upheavals in the librettos caused by the simultaneous presence of Cuzzoni and Faustina during the later years of the Royal Academy (1726–1728) have already been mentioned.

Another feature of London adaptations is abbreviation of the recitatives, which are far longer in *Almira*, *Rodrigo*, and *Agrippina* than in any of Handel's London operas. The difference is apparent at a glance if we compare Metastasio's complete text for *Siroe*, *Poro*, or *Ezio* with Handel's settings. In some of the Royal Academy operas, *Tamerlano* for instance, the recitatives remain substantial; but even at this period Handel sometimes did not set extensive passages that were printed in the librettos with a distinguishing sign. Later, from about 1731, the recitative was still more drastically compressed, both in revivals and in new operas, sometimes to the point of hopelessly obscuring the story. There can be little doubt about the reason for this: the audience was increasingly bored by recitative in a foreign language whose finer points it could not grasp.

The older librettos needed shortening in another respect; Handel's arias, and those of his contemporaries and juniors, were on a bigger musical scale than those of the seventeenth century. Something had to be done if the opera was not to last all night. Bussani's *Giulio Cesare* libretto, set by Antonio Sartorio for Venice in 1677, contains fifty-one arias; Haym's adaptation for Handel has thirty-three—a larger number, even so, than any of Handel's London operas except *Serse*. There was a significant redistribution of emphasis as well as a contraction: while the thirteen arias that Bussani gave to Curio, Nireno, and Rodisbe (a character suppressed by Haym) are all swept away, Caesar and Sesto have more arias in Handel's opera than in Sartorio's. Whether for dramatic or vocal reasons or both (probably both—Bussani gives all the characters except Rodisbe greater prominence than Sesto[5]), the principals obtain a higher proportion of the cake. The subplots are subordinated to the main action.[6]

The necessary pruning was not always carried out with a delicate hand. Sometimes an aria was simply removed, leaving a recitative followed by an exit. It is a back-handed tribute to the opera seria convention that this seldom fails to bring us up with a jerk. It seems not a relaxation of the form but a sacrifice of one of the props that hold it up. A piece of the design has fallen out. When the convention is abused —in this instance by the authors, but all too often by some clumsy modern hand—the framework protrudes like a broken bone.

It is clear from the letters of Rolli and others that a London libretto was sometimes the work of several hands, including Heidegger (the manager) and the principal singers as well as the theater poet and the composer. Rolli talks of being commissioned by the Academy in 1720 to shorten the libretto of *Onore e Maestà* for Amadei, reducing the recitatives but adding arias; he says the subject was suggested by Senesino and Durastanti, who were to sing the leading parts. Handel would only have been involved here in his capacity of musical director; and it is hard to imagine a man renowned for the defenestration of recalcitrant singers allowing them to choose his plots. Giuseppe Riva, the

---

[5] Sesto has three arias, compared with five for Achilla and Nireno, six for Caesar, Curio, Tolomeo, and Cornelia, and twelve for Cleopatra.

[6] Their elevation to vocal but not dramatic parity was a major weakness of the Cuzzoni-Faustina operas.

Modenese representative in London, in two letters to Muratori (1725–1726) speaks contemptuously of the Academy librettos as so much hackwork. He continues: "In England they want few recitatives, but thirty arias and one duet at least, distributed over the three acts. Their subject-matter must be straightforward, tender, heroic, Roman, Greek, or even Persian, and never Gothic or Longobard. . . . The duet should be at the end of the second Act, and between the two ladies."[7] Unfortunately Riva is a partial and inaccurate witness. He was a friend of Rolli, whose librettos he extolled at the expense of Haym's, whereas Rolli's are by far the more inept of the two. And much of what he says is untrue, at least of Handel's operas. Two of the four most recent, including the great success of the year in which he wrote, were titled *Flavio, Rè de'Longobardi* and *Rodelinda, Regina de'Longobardi.* So much for London's objection to the Longobards. Whether the subject matter could be described as straightforward is debatable; but if the reference is to the reduction of subplots and minor characters, this is a virtue. Handel's duets are scarcely ever between the two ladies; there is only one such (in *Ottone*) in all his operas up to this date. Moreover it does not appear, despite the testimony of Riva and Eisenschmidt, that his operas contain more arias than those of his contemporaries on the continent, though they certainly have much less recitative.

The extent of his personal influence on the preparation of his librettos is difficult to estimate, but was probably considerable. We have no relevant correspondence like his letters to Jennens about the oratorio *Belshazzar,* which show him deeply concerned with the dramatic design. There is evidence that this was also true of his operas, as we might expect. Several of the London works—*Rinaldo, Il Pastor Fido, Radamisto, Alcina*—contain words and music of arias composed for different contexts in Italy, and these can only have been inserted by the composer. More significantly, as Eisenschmidt has noted in connection with *Rodelinda, Lotario,* and several other operas, a comparison between Handel's librettos and their Italian originals[8] shows that many arias with a strong emotional content, especially those expressing grief or longing, were new in London; and it is in these arias above all that Handel brings

[7] Deutsch, p. 186.
[8] Always subject to the caveat that an intervening libretto may have disappeared.

the characters and their conflicts to life. We are probably safe in assuming that he was in some degree responsible for their inclusion, and for that of other episodes not present in the sources, such as the brilliantly effective opening of *Giulio Cesare* and *Ezio* and the built-up finales of *Ezio*, *Poro*, and *Ariodante*. Further search might yield many more examples. It is no accident that these are all points at which the music stretches the framework of opera seria.

Another modification characteristic of Handel had an important influence on the design of the libretto, and hence of the opera. This concerns the arioso at the start of an act, or sometimes of a new scene. Most contemporary librettos—those of Metastasio for instance—prefer to begin a scene with recitative; others, especially the older Venetian pieces, with a full aria. Handel wherever possible avoided both, and began an act either with an arioso or with an introductory or descriptive sinfonia. The significance of this lies in its structural possibilities. An arioso did not require the exit of the singer; like a sinfonia it could be used to build up towards a climax later in the scene, and so loosen one of the more tiresome bonds of the convention.[9]

It is difficult to be certain, without examining hundreds of librettos, to what extent Handel was an originator here. Ariosos had been common in the old Venetian opera, and there are several in *Agrippina*, including one at the start of the second scene of Act I.[10] But it is remarkable with what frequency a comparison between his London librettos and their sources shows these opening ariosos to be interpolations, made either by insertion, by the elevation of a few lines written for recitative, or by the omission of the second part of a da capo aria. For example, the initial ariosos in Act II of *Siroe*, Acts I and III of *Ariodante*, and Act I and Act II scene 3 of *Lotario* are insertions; those in Act II scenes 1 and 2 and Act III scene 2 of *Berenice* are cut down from da capo arias. In *Atalanta* three ariosos, including "Care selve" at the start of the opera, are the product of such substitution or abbreviation (as is the chorus that begins Act II). It is hard to believe that this consistent policy was not inspired by the composer who turned it to such advantage.

[9] For the musical consequences see pp. 52 and 135–136 below.
[10] Scene in the modern sense—a change of scenery, not the entry of a fresh character.

Whatever we may think of the London modifications as a whole (and it is difficult to defend all of them) the original Italian librettists were not all fools. The best of them were highly skilled writers for the theater. They had evolved over the years a method of reconciling the demands of the virtuoso singer—his da capo, his exit, and so on—with the need to tell a story in dramatic form. Each character is presented one facet at a time, aria by aria, until he stands complete. The principal figures have more arias and are more fully developed, but each attains, or should attain, a stature suitable to his importance in the story. The process is continuous throughout the opera, and it works on more than one level; for the order of the arias and the contrasts and tensions arising from their juxtaposition gradually tighten the various strands of the plot. If we can adjust ourselves to this scale and survey the opera in one glance, we sometimes find that the impression of a series of static episodes separated by capricious jerks is illusory. The entire opera is in motion.

This may sound far-fetched, and in many cases it manifestly fails to work. But not always. Let us see how it applies to one opera, *Alcina*, and at the same time observe Handel's response, without which the framework must remain a dead thing. *Alcina* is exceptional in that two scenes, one in the first act and one in the third, employ ballet and chorus; but while this facilitates appreciation by a modern audience, it does not alter the principles that underly the design and on which the characterization is built up. The text was adapted by an unknown author from an episode in Ariosto's *Orlando Furioso*.[11] It is the story of a sorceress who, like Circe, rules an enchanted island, seducing travelers and turning them into rocks, trees, and animals when she tires of them. She is genuinely in love with her current victim Ruggiero, who, under her spell, is equally obsessed with her. Ruggiero's wife Bradamante comes in search of him disguised as her own brother, a soldier, and is hospitably received on the island. In the course of the opera Ruggiero's eyes are opened, he breaks free from Alcina, and with the aid of superior magic destroys her spells and the island and rescues all her prisoners.

[11] Handel's libretto was certainly based on an earlier version, but this was not Antonio Marchi's *Alcina delusa da Ruggiero* (Venice, 1725), with which most authorities except Eisenschmidt have identified it.

Example 2

Alcina has six arias, two in each act. The first paints the amorous voluptuary; she tells Ruggiero to show the visitors round the island, and especially the place where they first declared their love. In the second she assures Ruggiero, who has grown jealous of the disguised Bradamante, that she is the same Alcina who will love him forever. So far she is the unashamed hedonist, a type Handel always drew with conspicuous sympathy. In Act II she becomes the woman scorned and then the sorceress practising her craft. On learning that Ruggiero means to desert her she sings an aria, "Ah! mio cor," whose two parts, as set by Handel, present the sharpest possible antithesis. It expresses with incomparable vividness the conflict between grief, love, injured pride, and vengeful fury that is tearing her apart, and the indecisive result is reflected in the da capo form. The first part is a slow C minor lament in triple time (example 2).

In the second part, an Allegro in E flat in common time, she tries to dispel her emotional dependence on Ruggiero—is she not Alcina,

Example 3

a queen and a magician?—but her heart betrays her, and the tragic
first part returns. This aria illustrates a feature hinted at above and
considered in more detail below,[12] Handel's method of making a dramatic point by modifying the design of the da capo aria, in this case
the treatment of the ritornellos. At the end of the first part the upper
strings, hitherto almost confined to the mournful detached chords of
example 2, break into a passionate yearning theme in a major key, un-
related to anything heard before, that seems to reveal emotions too
deep for words, in much the same way as the coda of Pamina's G minor
aria in *The Magic Flute* (example 3, p. 45). After the second part
Handel goes straight back to the unaccompanied first phrase of the

Example 4

12 See pp. 156 ff.

voice, omitting the original ritornello altogether. Alcina's mind, seething with thoughts of revenge, is suddenly overwhelmed by the recollection of her love (example 4).

At the end of Act II, standing before a statue of Circe, Alcina has an intensely dramatic accompanied recitative (the only one in the opera) invoking the spirits of hell to prevent Ruggiero's escape. But they have been paralyzed by superior powers and do not answer—a stroke wonderfully conveyed by Handel through the simple device of silencing the accompaniment:[13] she calls more and more desperately, her voice rising in strange angular intervals, into a musical void (example 5, p. 48). In the succeeding aria she addresses the spirits in a mixture of incredulity, bitterness, and despair, finally throwing down her magic wand in fury.

In Act III, confronted with Ruggiero, Alcina has another aria of divided emotions, but the balance has shifted and the desire for vengeance prevails. In the first part (Allegro 4/4, F major) she tells him contemptuously to go: when he returns he will be loaded with chains. The prospect of this momentarily revives her love, and in the second part (Largo 3/4, beginning on a quiet chord of D flat major) she makes one more appeal to him to stay, before her threats and anger return with the da capo. But Ruggiero defeats the supernatural forces on which she relies, and her sixth aria is a lament: nothing is left but tears and a hopeless longing to drown her sorrows. Her final appearance is in a trio with Ruggiero and Bradamante. Stripped of her dignity, she tries to detain them with weeping and blandishments, moved (she says) not by love or jealousy but by desire for their happiness and pity for the dangers they will meet on their journey. They see through her schemes, and when Ruggiero smashes her magic urn she and her island vanish for ever.

From this material, in music of exceptional psychological subtlety, Handel has created a tragic heroine whose character grows in human richness as her fortunes decline, so that her fate is profoundly moving. She has the stature of a queen, the passion of a woman in love, the evil glitter of a sorceress, and the pathos of pride brought low, for she can

---

[13] The concertino violins double the voice, presumably to keep the singer in tune.

48

Example 5

command everything except the love of the man she wants. Her entire part, outside the recitative, is bounded by the confines of da capo form.

This is not all. The other six characters, who include a contrasted pair of lovers and a boy in search of his lost father (one of Alcina's earlier victims), are drawn with the same sure feeling for individuality. Ruggiero too grows in the course of the opera. At first he is so completely under Alcina's spell that he takes the disguised Bradamante, his own wife, for a rival, refusing to believe her when she tells him who she is. When the film is removed from his eyes, he dismisses her as another of Alcina's phantoms, till she begs him to kill her. His dawning suspicion that she may indeed be his wife, and the mixture of tenderness and self-reproach this induces, is conveyed in the exquisite aria "Mi lusinga."

In the next scene Ruggiero has a two-mood aria of a different type from Alcina's. He is playing for time and he assures her that he is indeed faithful, adding in an ironical aside at the cadences: "But not to you." The aria in which he says farewell to the island, "Verdi prati," has one of Handel's most famous melodies. Carestini, the castrato for whom it was written, has earned a black mark in history for rejecting it when it was sent him out of context. He has perhaps been judged too severely, for the overwhelming effect of this aria in the theater arises precisely from the context in which it comes. (This is true of a great many of Handel's opera arias.) Ruggiero, happily reunited with Bradamante and about to return home, looks for the last time on the earthly paradise where he has enjoyed so many happy hours. The prospect fills him with a half-involuntary nostalgia that Handel's music depicts very simply—there is not a trace of vocal display, which of course is why Carestini complained—but with extraordinary intensity. No wonder Bradamante seeks to hurry him away. In the last act, where his only aria is the exuberant "Stà nell'Ircana,"[14] he is the hero restored, the triumphant rescuer of the oppressed.

The order of the arias in *Alcina* opens the way to many strokes of dramatic irony. One of the grandest is the placing of Alcina's vain conjuration of the spirits immediately after "Verdi prati," reinforced by

[14] See p. 22 above.

Example 6

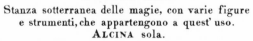

SCENA XIII.

Stanza sotterranea delle magie, con varie figure
e strumenti, che appartengono a quest' uso.
ALCINA sola.

the plunge from the serene unbroken E major of its long ritornello into the jagged darkness of B minor. This is typical of Handel's method of marking a change of scene through the tonality (example 6).[15]

There is a very different type of irony a little earlier, when Alcina's heart softens towards the boy Oberto and she promises that he shall see his father again, just before the news of Ruggiero's proposed flight reaches her and converts her once more into a demon. All through the opera the words and actions of the characters throw an oblique and often ironical light on each other. The trivial and intermittent love affair between Alcina's flighty sister Morgana and the easy-going general Oronte places Alcina's consuming passion for Ruggiero, the latter's love for his wife, and Oberto's devotion to his father in continual relief. This is not an opera in which various characters happen to fall in love; it is an opera about the nature of love itself, as revealed in their actions. Its theme is not magic but the human heart.

The music and the drama interlock throughout, not least in the careful gradation of climaxes. Each of the first two acts has a big climax near the beginning and another at the end. In Act I there is the spectacular revelation of Alcina's court in the second scene,[16] with its life of endless pleasure celebrated in a seductive sequence of chorus and ballet movements, and at the end Morgana's brilliant aria "Tornami a vagheggiar," rejoicing that she has found a new lover in the disguised Bradamante—a complex ironical situation typical alike of Ariosto, Handel, and the opera seria convention. This aria should never be sung by Alcina, in whose mouth it is completely out of character. Handel gave it to her in a truncated revival when he had no soprano for Morgana. Chrysander notes both versions but gives preference to the inferior substitute.

Act II begins with a striking scene in which Ruggiero learns the truth about Alcina's enchantments. Handel gives him two ariosos, both marked "Largo," linked by recitative. In the first, "Col celarvi," Ruggiero complains of Alcina's cruelty in absenting herself even for a moment. This is interrupted by Melisso, Bradamante's guardian (bass), who

[15] See pp. 127–128 below.
[16] The scene change must have been breathtaking in the eighteenth-century theater; see p. 124 below.

appears in the form of Ruggiero's old tutor Atlante and rebukes him for abandoning his noble destiny for wanton idleness. He puts a magic ring on Ruggiero's finger, and the splendid hall of Alcina's palace changes to "a horrid desart Place" during the ritornello of the second arioso—Handel called it "cavata" in the autograph—in which Ruggiero asks in astonishment what portent has restored his vision.

Example 7

There is still no exit: Melisso replies in another recitative, and the scene builds up to *his* aria and exit, while Ruggiero remains on the stage. This is a good instance of the flexibility conferred by the use of arioso; the design is varied and the tension prolonged. Ruggiero is the only character in the opera who is allowed to express himself other than in a full da capo aria.[17]

The climax at the end of Act II, Alcina's despair when the spirits

[17] "Verdi prati" is a rondo.

desert her, has already been described. That of Act III is the trio, a fully concerted movement placed at the decisive point of the action, which is then resolved in another choral and ballet sequence as Alcina's victims return in wonder to their human shape. It is notable—but has not always been noted by stage directors—how carefully both ballet scenes are integrated with the action. Between the main climaxes are many minor ones, each represented by an aria. Every aria thus serves three purposes, in addition to its musical functions of diverting the ear and providing a vehicle for the singer: it develops the characterization, it marks a point of advance in the story, and through its relationship to what precedes and follows—whether in dramatic irony, tonality, or other means of contrast—it acts as a joint in the articulation of the whole opera.

The libretto of *Alcina* is not perfect. There are a few loose ends left over from its pre-Handelian original, and one almost unactable scene between Alcina, Oberto, and a lion. Alcina gives the boy a spear to kill the hungry beast, which promptly lies down and licks his feet; whereupon Oberto, with remarkable perception, recognizes it as his father. But this recitative can be cut, and it is hardly an exaggeration to claim that music and drama interact and play into each other's hands as fruitfully as in the masterpieces of Mozart and Da Ponte. Nor is *Alcina* the only Handel opera of which this can be said. The claim is difficult to substantiate without a performance of the whole work. But that is precisely the point: Handel's design *is* the whole work. There is a complete commercial recording of *Alcina*, including one aria in the first act that has never been published; but the full dramatic experience cannot be communicated outside the theater.

CHAPTER 5

⚜⚜⚜⚜⚜⚜⚜⚜⚜⚜⚜

Heroic Operas

Handel's operas can be separated into categories according to the dominant temper of the librettos. The divisions are not watertight, but they reflect a broadly valid distinction, and this has nothing to do with the chronological sequence. The largest group, to which twenty-four out of thirty-nine surviving operas belong, may be called heroic or dynastic. What distinguishes them is not so much the rank of the characters (almost everyone in opera seria belongs to a royal or noble family), or the motives that govern their conduct, or the tacit assumption that the fate of nations turns on the private whim of their rulers, but the solemn and often grandiose spirit in which all this is treated by the authors. No representative of the common people appears; if the monarch is overthrown, it is by some rival for personal reasons such as ambition, jealousy, or lust—whether for power or for the monarch's wife, sister, or daughter. Love and statecraft are the themes of heroic opera; they are exercised by means of copious intrigue. The characters are torn by a conflict between amorous and political motives, and they have a great deal to say about outraged honor. Indeed one could almost classify them according to their conception of the meaning of honor.

The stories are derived from some classical or historical source, and many of the characters are historical persons. The librettists seem to have prided themselves on supplying authentic detail, for they generally point out in their Argument how much of the plot is founded on fact. Almost the first remark of Julius Caesar in Handel's opera is "I came, I saw, I conquered." The most recent stories are *Riccardo*

Primo and *Tamerlano*, whose events are placed in the years 1191 and 1402 respectively. The historical Tamerlano was thus separated from Handel by no more than the span that divides us from Charles I and Cromwell. There was of course no serious attempt to follow history, which would have been impossible in opera seria, though a didactic intention to hold up certain figures as models, and others as awful warnings, was certainly present in the minds of some librettists. Entertainment was not considered incompatible with instruction.

The plots are full of family feuds and vendettas, palace revolutions, lost heirs, disguises, and mistaken identities. Often so much has happened before the curtain rises that a listener who failed to read the Argument in his libretto (never reprinted by Chrysander) might become hopelessly lost, and once or twice he would not be much the wiser if he had read it. There is a good deal of fighting on and off stage, with sieges, sorties, and the sacking of cities; the spectacular breach of the walls of Oxidraca in *Alessandro* was such a success with the public that a similar episode, using the same scenery and mechanical effects, seems to have been introduced into *Riccardo Primo*, *Lotario*, and even an opera by Veracini based on Shakespeare's *As You Like It*.[1] The characters are presented in black and white terms, the men noble or nefarious, the women virtuous and long-suffering or seething with ambition and conspiracy. The composer was expected to supply the light and shade, and it is surprising how consistently Handel does bring these puppets to life. But he is sometimes baffled by the malign unscrupulousness of a tyrant or the perverse generosity of a hero whose conduct is such that one wonders how he can survive in a world so fraught with hazard and treason. The answer is that if he did not the opera would come to an abrupt end.

It is this type of heroic libretto that has earned opera seria its reputation for remoteness and absurdity. The trouble lies less in the convention than in its abuse by particular librettists, and in our habit

[1] It was not uncommon for the same sets to reappear in several operas; the librettos often give a clue to this. The grove of palm and cypress trees in *Poro*, *Orlando*, and the 1731 revival of *Rinaldo*, the shepherds' cottages or "Champion Country with a delightful Village" in *Pastor Fido*, *Tolomeo*, *Orlando*, and *Atalanta*, and the military encampments in half-a-dozen operas were probably served out of stock. When new scenery was made, it was usually mentioned in the press announcements.

of assessing the libretto apart from the music. The basic material is not so different from that of many romantic operas, including the early works of Verdi—though that may be thought no high recommendation. The exchange of children in *Il Trovatore* is anticipated in *Faramondo*, and the quixotic honor of the Spaniards in *Scipione* is no more extreme than in *Ernani*. What we do find in opera seria is an attempt to turn the whole thing into a system, with the plot and the characters, as well as the recitative-aria design, subject to a narrow set of rules. This development, implicit in the seventeenth century, culminated in the work of Metastasio. Although Handel set no more than three of Metastasio's librettos (during the years 1728–1731), the results tell us a great deal about the qualities of both men, and a comparison of these three operas with Handel's other works in the heroic class is illuminating.

Metastasio was a distinguished poet, ranked by his contemporaries with Homer and Dante; his self-appointed task was to reform and purify the opera seria libretto. The clarity of his language, free from extravagance and bombast, and his expressive imagery offered composers a text admirably suited to musical setting. He rejected certain elements in the libretto that had survived from the seventeenth century, in particular the extravagant use of stage machines and scenic spectacle, dancing, all manifestations of the supernatural, and the adulteration of the heroic temper with comic episodes, so characteristic of Venetian opera. In his hierarchy of the theater the playwright ranked far above the scene painter, with the musician perhaps in the middle.[2] His librettos aimed at dignity and a lofty humanism in the spirit of his age, and were designed to present a standard of conduct suitable to princes, based on the classical Roman virtues.

It is no charge against Metastasio that his librettos are artificial. But whether because he was too much the moral doctrinaire, or lacked the power of conceiving characters in the round, or was content to follow the practice of his age and think in terms of scenes rather than whole dramas, in removing real and imaginary impurities from the opera seria libretto he undermined the one thing that mattered and

---

[2] Compare the quarrel between Ben Jonson and Inigo Jones about priorities in the Stuart masque.

always matters in opera, consistent characterization. The machinery is smooth and perfectly oiled, but it is impossible to believe that any human beings could go through the motions prescribed by Metastasio. His creatures are as flat as cardboard, and as easily bent: the situation governs the character, rather than the other way round. It was Metastasio's work, not the tyranny of the singers, that made Gluck's reforms inevitable if opera was to survive.

There is a striking parallel a century later in the work of Scribe, a far inferior poet but again a puppet-master rather than a dramatist. In the librettos of both, the characters, instead of spinning the plot, are maneuvered into a series of situations that, however effective in isolation, do not add up to a dramatic entity because they are linked by no thread of credible human conduct. Metastasio and Scribe were immensely popular, and the source of innumerable operas all over Europe. Both founded their librettos on a stock pattern; both favored subjects with a strong political content; each was proud of his status as a man of letters; each had a favorite composer whose operas won universal success in their day but have not stood the test of time—Hasse in one case, Meyerbeer in the other. And it is no accident that the hundreds of serious operas based on the work of these two librettists, the most admired in operatic history, do not include a single acknowledged masterpiece.[3]

The composer who came nearest to surmounting this barrier was undoubtedly Handel. All three of his Metastasio operas—*Siroe, Poro,* and *Ezio*—are full of superb music; indeed they contain scarcely a dull aria. Handel was sensitive to the quality of poetry, as his Milton and Dryden settings prove, and to the dramatic possibilities of a strong situation; hence the many episodes of genius scattered about his least successful operas. He was not dependent on the supernatural, spectacular, and comic elements that Metastasio eschewed, though they were the basis of some of his finest works; he was capable of composing a great opera in the heroic style. But his great glory as a dramatic composer is his sense of character, of men and women struggling to maintain themselves against the harshness of destiny; and he was hamstrung by

[3] Scribe's comedies are another matter, since comic opera draws its strength as much from intrigue as from character.

the frigid and convoluted maneuvering of Metastasio's creatures, a much graver obstacle than the operatic conventions to which they were bound.

Metastasio's assertion of the primacy of letters was sure to cause strain with a composer unwilling to subordinate his muse to the librettist's. We are often told that Handel's abridgment of the recitative weakens the Metastasio librettos. If they are read as literature, this is indisputable; but if we view the result as musical drama—opera—the conclusion seems more doubtful. Metastasio's leisurely progress, with acres of recitative before and between every aria, very few ariosos or duets, and characters going through set moves like pieces on a political chessboard, conflicts with Handel's desire to get on with the story and express its vicissitudes and conflicts so far as possible by musical means. Handel tightens the action in Act II of *Poro* by suppressing Metastasio's first four scenes (using one of the arias later) and beginning at once with Cleofide's reception of the Macedonian army on the Hydaspes and the battle, represented in a military symphony. He cuts the long preliminary recitative in the first scene of *Ezio* and launches the opera with a bang as the hero returns triumphant from his victory over Attila in the middle of the overture.[4]

There is a significant change in the temper of these librettos, especially *Poro*. Metastasio stresses Alexander's political virtues; Handel shifts the emphasis to what interests him more, the story of love, jealousy, and despair. He and his London poet altered the words of the second duet for Poro and Cleofide (during the battle in Act II) from a prayer to the gods for protection to a passionate renewal of their love, and added a third duet at the end of the opera, followed not by Metastasio's coro celebrating Alexander as hero but by a new ensemble, organically linked to the duet, in praise of love. *Siroe* and *Ezio* likewise received new finales in which an emotional reaction replaces Metastasio's detached moral. Where Metastasio was more interested in abstraction, Handel goes every time for the feelings of the individual.

He is brilliantly successful with the tangled passions of Poro and Cleofide. But otherwise it was a losing battle. Handel's music exposes

[4] See p. 131 below.

the fustian in Metastasio; it cannot replace it. The trouble with Metastasio's heroes is not their improbable nobility but their fundamental lack of principle; acting on the assumption that the end justifies the means and blood is thicker than honor, they again and again cut morally deplorable figures, an impression that Metastasio's preoccupation with dignity and lofty sentiments cannot fail to underline. All the chief characters in *Siroe* behave with a mixture of sycophancy, vindictiveness, untruthfulness, and irresolution that makes any sustained interest, let alone sympathy, almost impossible. Alexander the Great in *Poro* is held up as a paragon of virtue, and he does show a surprising clemency towards every type of treachery on the part of his soldiers and allies. Yet he is not above trying to blackmail Cleofide into marrying him on the ground that this is the only way he (of all men) can appease his army; and at the end of the opera he congratulates Poro, who has been caught planning a double murder, on his preservation of a royal soul through all the vicissitudes of fortune.

In *Ezio* the relationship between Massimo and his daughter Fulvia is incredible. Massimo involves Fulvia in a peculiarly dishonorable plot to murder the Emperor and lay the blame on the national hero Ezio; Fulvia, though she loves Ezio, prefers to shield her father to the point of pretending, in Ezio's presence, to be in love with the Emperor. Handel was outstandingly successful with father-daughter relationships in *Tamerlano, Ariodante, Deidamia, Joshua*, and elsewhere; but he could do little here except give Fulvia the most ravishing music. Metastasio was one of the worst offenders in the contrivance of unconvincing happy ends and the multiplication of simile arias, and he may have been the originator of a type of aria that delighted parodists a century later. Just before the end of *Ezio* the captain of the Praetorian Guard, Varo, hears a noise of revolution and battle offstage. He stops to deliver an elaborate aria, which Handel set with trumpet obbligato, asking himself over and over again why he lingers when the Emperor and empire are in mortal danger.

These weaknesses, though not of course confined to Metastasio, are not (apart from the statutory happy end) endemic to opera seria, as we have seen with *Alcina*, or even to the heroic-dynastic type. The work of Metastasio's predecessors is often feeble, and it seldom if ever

approaches his felicity in language. But we have these forgotten librettists to thank for the fact that Handel's heroic operas, despite a high
proportion of failures, do include several masterpieces or near-master-
pieces. The plots of *Radamisto* and *Tamerlano* may be intricate for
modern taste, but the central conflicts ring true, the different strands
are skilfully woven together, and the motives of the characters (until
the final scene) are reasonably clear and consistent, so that the music
can develop a high emotional pressure. The crucial point is that the
finest of these heroic operas have a basically simple theme, some central facet of human experience, on which Handel's imagination could
seize: the eternal seductiveness of Cleopatra in *Giulio Cesare*, which he
expresses with an artistry comparable to Shakespeare's, the mutual devotion of a married couple in face of political oppression and overwhelming odds in *Radamisto* and *Rodelinda*, the conflict between a father's
unbending pride and his love for his daughter in *Tamerlano*, and the
self-sacrifice of a wife for her husband in *Admeto*. These operas have
their weaker moments, and *Admeto* is flawed by a second plot that
assumes too much prominence for extraneous reasons; but they possess
that spiritual grandeur and unity that is a property of the highest art.
It is no accident that precisely the same themes have inspired some of
the greatest operas in other periods and conventions—Monteverdi's
Coronation of Poppea, Beethoven's *Fidelio*, Verdi's *Simon Boccanegra*,
and Gluck's *Alceste*.

These operas of Handel are genuinely heroic. The principal characters belong to the same order of nobility as Beethoven's Leonora and
Verdi's Otello, because Handel presents them in their strength and
weakness as human beings grappling with the problems of life and
death. This power of projecting himself into his characters underlies
his whole dramatic method, in oratorio as well as opera. The range of
his sympathy seems unlimited;[5] he can identify with men and women
of every type in any situation. The libretto may offer him emperor or
clown, soldier or princess, conspirator or matriarch, tyrant or flirt;
Handel sees a human being in love, hope, or misfortune, at grips with

[5] It extends to comedy; see chapter 7 below.

his passions or his enemies. Donald Grout in his *Short History of Opera*[6] has put this point particularly well. After excluding purely descriptive pieces he continues: "The number and variety of these arias is so great, and the power of capturing the most subtle nuances of feeling so astounding, that one is tempted to believe there is no emotion of which humanity is capable that has not found musical expression somewhere in Handel's operas." This capacity to express suffering on a heroic scale Grout describes as "the direct emanation of Handel's spirit, expressed in music with an immediacy that has no parallel outside Beethoven"; and he concludes: "We are moved by the spectacle of suffering, but our compassion is mingled with admiration at suffering so nobly endured, with pride that we ourselves belong to a species capable of such heroism."

That is a fair definition of our response to tragedy in all dramatic art. This quality appears very early in Handel's work, though only fitfully before *Radamisto*. We find it in Almira's jealousy in his first opera; in Claudio's aria in *Silla* when he thinks he is to be thrown to the lions; and again and again where we meet a rejected, misunderstood, or deserted heroine, a hero betrayed by treachery or languishing in prison, a proud ruler humbled by misfortune. A character's loss of love or liberty scarcely ever failed to bring the greatest out of Handel. That is another reason why even the weakest of his operas contain wonderful episodes, and why we cannot ignore them without missing something of value. The muddled and often ridiculous libretto of *Arminio* has a scene in which the hero, led in chains to the scaffold, contemplates what he calls "the proud theatre of death." As in Caesar's famous monologue before Pompey's tomb in *Giulio Cesare*, Handel writes a superb accompanied recitative, full of chromatic inflections, that expresses with piercing intensity the brevity of life and the futility of mortal hopes. The heroic librettos are full of situations like this, and they constantly inspire music of this quality. Such scenes possess something of the lapidary power of the great soliloquies in Shakespeare's tragedies. They are at once individual and universal.

[6] New York, 1947, pp. 174–175.

Example 8

bra ca _ra di_ mia spo_ sa, deh! ri _ po_sa, deh! ri_

po_sa,e lie_ta a_spet_ta la ven_det_ta, la ven_det_ta che fa_rò! om_bra ca_ _ ra,

om _ bra ca_ra di mia spo_sa, deh! ri _po_sa,e lie _ ta a_spet_ta la ven_det_ta,

It is when the libretto permits a sustained response on this level that Handel outsoars the convention and presents us across the centuries with a great work of art. In the heroic operas of the early Royal Academy years, especially *Radamisto, Giulio Cesare, Tamerlano,* and *Rodelinda,* almost every character is drawn with equal penetration. The central figures of *Radamisto* are two married couples, whose emotional predicament transcends the dynastic background of the plot. Tiridate, though he has a devoted wife in Polissena, lusts after his sister-in-law Zenobia, the wife of Polissena's brother Radamisto; he therefore invades Radamisto's kingdom and defeats him in battle. Zenobia throws herself into the river Araxes to escape capture, and Radamisto, believing her dead, pours out his heart in one of the profoundest expressions of grief in the history of opera (example 8, pp. 62–63). The chromaticism is typical of Handel's style at all periods; but after leaving Italy he reserved it for utterances of intense personal anguish, where its impact is all the more overwhelming. Most of these contexts occur in the operas.[7]

Polissena loves her husband Tiridate and frustrates Radamisto's plan to assassinate him, but in the end his brutality transforms her from a long-suffering wife into a tigress for revenge. Two quotations, each addressed to Tiridate, may give an idea of the range of her character. Both arias dispense with an opening ritornello, suggesting the spontaneous nature of her reaction. In Act I, when Tiridate brusquely dismisses her, she can think only of the grief of separation from him (example 9). In Act III Tiridate captures Radamisto, and despite Polissena's pleas for mercy orders his execution. This is too much for her; she turns and rends him. In context, after she has defended Tiridate through thick and thin, even against her wronged brother, the effect of her outburst is devastating (example 10, pp. 66–67).

Giulio Cesare has a large cast, all of whom come to life in their music. Caesar himself is as much a lover as a conqueror; Tolomeo, the second alto castrato, is feline, vengeful, and treacherous; the Egyptian general Achilla, a bass, represents the bluffer type of villainy; Pompey's son Sesto is an impetuous boy in his teens (Handel wrote the part for a female soprano) who burns to avenge his father and defend his

---

[7] There are however several striking examples in his last oratorio, *Jephtha.*

Example 9

Example 10

barbaro! parti rò, barbaro! parti rò, mà sdegno poi ver-

-rà, che a_mo_re can_ge_rà,

che a_mo_re can_ge_rà tut_to in fie_rez_za;

mà sde_gno poi ver_rà, che a_mo_re can_ge_rà,

mother's honor. But the finest characters are the two women, Pompey's widow Cornelia, a tragic figure who at her first entrance is confronted with the head of her murdered husband, and the young queen Cleopatra. Cleopatra has eight arias, besides two magnificent accompanied recitatives and a duet. They show her in an infinite variety of mood, teasing her brother Tolomeo about his love affairs, confident in the compelling power of her beauty, setting out to seduce Caesar with a tableau of the Muses on Mount Parnassus, praying to Venus to aid her amorous designs, uttering a more urgent prayer when Caesar is attacked by conspirators, lamenting her fate and threatening to haunt Tolomeo when he has captured her and she thinks Caesar is dead, and finally rejoicing in her conquest of the conqueror of the world. Unlike Cornelia she cannot be described as tragic or heroic, but she is one of the great characters of opera, an immortal sex-kitten whose emotions, if ephemeral, are obsessive while they last.[8]

In *Tamerlano* there are again two alto castrato roles in sharp contrast—Tamerlano himself, a mental rather than a physical sadist who tortures his victims with threats, and Andronico, a sympathetic hero torn between loyalty to his ally Tamerlano and love for Asteria, the daughter of the fallen Emperor Bajazet, whom Tamerlano covets for himself. There will be more to say about this opera in connection with Handel's method of expressing the cumulative and interacting tensions that build up between the characters.[9] An unusual feature is that Bajazet, one of the biggest parts, was written for a tenor. His indomitable pride makes his position as a captive intolerable, the more so when he discovers Tamerlano's designs on his daughter; at the last throw he thwarts the tyrant by committing suicide. His music throughout is magnificent; some of it bears a startling resemblance to certain movements in Bach's *St. Matthew Passion* (which had not yet been written, and which Handel could not have known if it had). The aria (example 11, pp. 70–71) in which Bajazet, believing that Asteria intends to marry Tamerlano and share his throne, tells her that she will see her father die at her feet is the most striking of several examples.[10] It is curious that in this aria

[8] For quotations see pp. 182–183 and 193 below.
[9] See pp. 144–146 below.
[10] The upper notes for the voice are the original.

Handel borrows two motives from two different movements in his early oratorio *Le Resurrezione*, Lucifer's aria "Caddi è ver" and the duet "Dolci chiodi." The associative significance of his self-borrowings is a subject that awaits investigation.

The next opera, *Rodelinda*, has another fine tenor part in the vicious but weak and finally conscience-stricken Grimoaldo, who has deprived Bertarido of his throne in the hope of possessing his wife Rodelinda. There is a superficial resemblance to the plot of *Fidelio*, with a husband and wife separated by a tyrant and a great prison scene in the last act; but Rodelinda, unlike other Handel heroines, does not disguise herself as a boy. Several of these heroic operas are concerned with a married couple torn apart by violence or misunderstanding, and since the wife always shows the utmost gallantry in braving danger on her husband's behalf we are reminded of the rescue operas of the French Revolution period, whose greatest example is of course *Fidelio* itself. There is, however, the vital difference that in Handel's librettos the political background remains shadowy: his prison scenes are profoundly moving, but they never suggest the concentration camp. The prisoner is not a symbol for humanity.

Handel's women are if anything an even more remarkable portrait gallery than his men, and he attained this mastery sooner. Many of the early castrato heroes, including Rinaldo, tend to be stiff and wooden; some, like Rodrigo and Silla, are thoroughly unsympathetic as well. But *Rodrigo*, the second of his surviving operas, has two beautifully drawn heroines. Florinda has been seduced by Rodrigo and had a child by him; throughout the opera she seeks to avenge this outrage to her honor, among other things by promoting civil war. In Act II Rodrigo's wife Esilena, though she still loves her husband, offers to give him up to Florinda if this will bring the country peace. The scene for the two women has a wonderful and very simple climax: Esilena makes her offer in an aria beginning without ritornello with the words "Egli è tuo"—"He is yours" (example 12, p. 72). The musical phrase is familiar from Handel's re-use of it to the words "Comfort ye" in *Messiah*. As with other such parallels there is a clear emotional link—the idea of consolation or self-sacrifice—between the two passages, though this may not have been consciously present in Handel's mind. Many later

Example 11

Example 12

works in addition to *Radamisto* and *Giulio Cesare* contain two fully developed heroines of contrasted type, either of whom would lend distinction to any ordinary opera.[11]

There are plenty of noble characters and great arias in the heroic operas after 1724–1725, though none of them attains the consistent level of the masterpieces of those years. The fault appears to lie in the quality of the librettos, the awkward constitution of Handel's company with its rival prima donnas, and eventually the pressure exerted by the changing taste of the audience. It seems improbable that the arrangers of Handel's London librettos (with the possible exception of Haym, his collaborator in the best Academy operas) understood the nature of his genius, and in particular its need to fasten on some fundamental conflict if it was to flower to the full. Every one of his heroic operas after *Rodelinda,* including the three on texts by Metastasio, has some central flaw in characterization or construction that the music cannot quite redeem. There is little or no decline in invention, and nearly always at least one character—Lucejo in *Scipione,* Costanza in *Riccardo Primo,* the tyrant Berengario (another tenor part) in *Lotario*—rises to memorable stature while the others remain half paralyzed by the limitations of the libretto.

The most tantalizing example is *Admeto,* based partly on the *Alcestis* of Euripides and partly on a complex tangle of disguises and mistaken identities in a Venetian libretto of 1660. Handel's response to classical Greek themes, most notably in *Semele, Hercules,* and the character of Medea in *Teseo,* was so powerful that we must regret his lack of opportunity to try conclusions with Clytemnestra and Orestes. His

[11] For example *Agrippina, Teseo, Amadigi,* and *Orlando.* For reasons already noted, the Cuzzoni-Faustina operas (with the partial exception of *Admeto*) are less successful in this respect.

treatment of the Euripides half of *Admeto* has the noble simplicity of Gluck allied to a far richer musical invention. But this clashes with the involutions of the subplot, and the dramatic unity is fractured. Alcestis sacrifices her life for her husband, as in the legend, but after her rescue by Hercules she turns intriguer and brings needless troubles on her own head. She is no sooner out of Hades than she disguises herself as a man in order to test Admeto's fidelity. Since he still thinks her dead, he not unnaturally begins to show interest in another woman. The librettist was not content with this absurdity. In Act II Alcestis grows madly jealous without cause while Admeto is mourning her death; in Act III, when his courting of Antigona might be thought grounds for resentment, she warbles amiably and at great length about birds. There is one amusing scene, beautifully set by Handel, in which Admeto, overheard by his wife, has a love duet with the wrong woman just before the end of the opera; but this belongs to a different world from the classical grandeur of the opening scenes of the first two acts, and Handel despite some marvelous music does not quite succeed in bridging the dichotomy.

Once or twice the sheer force of his imagination comes near to redeeming a flawed libretto. This happens with two of the Metastasio operas, *Poro* and *Ezio,* and with *Sosarme,* which began life under the title of *Fernando Rè di Castiglia.* For some reason unknown the scene was changed from Coimbra in Portugal during the Middle Ages to Sardis in the time of the Medes and Persians after Handel had composed two acts of the music. It is difficult to feel enthusiasm for the dynastic intrigues and inadequate motivation of the plot, and impossible to discover a central theme. Yet Handel reproduces the emotion of the characters in each situation with such intensity that the score, if not the drama, haunts the memory. He endows the bass Altomaro, whose all but motiveless malignity spins most of the plot, with music of ravishing beauty, as when he compares his illegitimate grandson to a mentally confused butterfly (example 13, pp. 74–75). This was adapted from one of Polifemo's arias in *Aci, Galatea e Polifemo,* composed twenty-five years earlier in Italy, and Handel was doubtless drawing on his musical capital to counteract the weakness of the drama. This seems to have been a regular response to a stiff libretto or a rebarbative situation; it can give us a musical feast, but scarcely an artistic whole. As already

Example 13

_der,_____ far_fal_la con_fu_sa fra l'òm_bre e gl'òr

ro _ _ _ _ ri già spen_ta la fa _ ce non sà mai go_

der, non sà mai go_der.

remarked, it is common in simile arias: two of the loveliest and most richly wrought pieces in *Poro*, "Senza procelle" and "Son confusa pastorella," have no perceptible link with their context. In *Sosarme* it may also reflect Handel's pleasure in writing for a new singer, Antonio Montagnana, a genuine bass and not a baritone like Boschi, for whom most of the Royal Academy bass parts had been composed. *Sosarme*, though it has been broadcast and recorded, has never been revived on the stage since 1734. But it would be rash to exclude the possibility that, like other unpromising Handel operas, it might confound expectation by coming to life.

CHAPTER 6

✿✿✿✿✿✿✿✿✿✿

Magic Operas

The second group of Handel's operas has magic as a principal ingredient of the plot. There are only five of them, and three are early
works composed before the age of thirty; but they are important as a
recognized variant of opera seria and because they reveal certain facets
of Handel's genius more fully than the heroic operas. This was the
type of libretto that gave most scope to the visual aspect of the baroque
theater—the elaborate transformation scenes achieved by quick changes
of scenery and lighting, the machines in which gods and monsters could
descend or rise, the waterworks department with its live fountains, and
so on. The scene-painters came into their own, and so did the ballet.
During Handel's first years in London the Haymarket Theatre appears
to have kept a permanent group of dancers, though probably not a large
one.[1] They may have been used, in association with supers and machines,
to impersonate the numerous spirits, genii, and dragons required on the
stage.

   Before considering the effect of this on the music it is instructive
to run through the stage directions of *Rinaldo* and discover what sort
of entertainment was offered to the eye. In the first scene Argante
emerges from the besieged city of Jerusalem "in a Triumphal Chariot,
the Horses white and led in by arm'd Blackamoors. He comes forward
attended by a great Number of Horse and Foot Guards." Steele com-

---

[1] The advertisements for *Amadigi* in 1715 mention "variety of Dancing," and
dancers are named for various performances of *Rinaldo* in 1711 and 1717 (when
Marie Sallé made her London début as a child).

plained in the *Spectator*[2] that the promised horse-drawn chariot did not appear, though a large contingent of sparrows and chaffinches did. Armida makes her first entrance "in the Air, in a Chariot drawn by two huge Dragons, out of whose Mouths issue Fire and Smoke." Later in the act "a black Cloud descends, all fill'd with dreadful Monsters spitting Fire and Smoke on every side. The Cloud covers Almirena and Armida, and carries 'em up swiftly into the Air, leaving in their Place, two frightful Furies, who having grinn'd and mock'd Rinaldo, sink down, and disappear." The Furies were presumably human, whereas the dragons were part of a machine with a boy inside to operate the pyrotechnics.[3] We learn without surprise that fire-fighting appliances were kept ready in the theater for emergency.

Act II opens on "a Prospect of a Calm and Sunshiny Sea, with a Boat at Anchor close upon the Shore; at the Helm of the Boat sets a Spirit, in the Shape of a lovely Woman. Two Mermaids are seen Dancing up and down in the Water." These are the Sirens of Handel's score, who captivate Rinaldo with the aria "Il vostro maggio"; they sing in unison, dancing at the same time (if they obey instructions).[4] Presently the boat sails off into the open sea with the Spirit and Rinaldo on board. In the second scene, "a Delightful Garden in the Enchanted Palace of Armida," the sorceress has to change her shape on stage no fewer than six times.

That is nothing to what happens in Act III. The first scene reveals

a dreadful Prospect of a Mountain, horridly steep, and rising from the Front of the Stage, to the utmost Height of the most backward Part of the Theatre; Rocks, and Caves, and Waterfalls, are seen upon the Ascent, and on the Top appear the blazing Battlements of the Enchanted Palace, Guarded by a great Number of Spirits, of various Forms and Aspects; In the midst of the Wall is seen a Gate, with several Arches supported by Pillars of Chrystal, Azure, Emeralds, and all sorts of precious Stones. At the Foot of the Mountain is discover'd the Magicians Cave.

[2] March 16, 1711.
[3] According to Steele he failed to keep his head down.
[4] But it is possible that the Spirit sang the aria, as happened in the 1731 revival when there were no mermaids.

This is the Christian Magician who supplies the white magic. Goffredo and his army make two assaults on the stronghold. On the first occasion, without waiting to consult the Magician, they draw their swords and charge half way up, where they "are stopp'd by a Row of ugly Spirits, who start up before 'em; The Soldiers, frighted, endeavour to run back, but are cut off in their Way by another Troop, who start up below 'em. In the midst of their Confusion, the Mountain opens and swallows 'em up, with Thunder, Lightning, and amazing Noises."

The survivors retire "in great Confusion," and take the proper precaution of obtaining magic wands from the Magician.

> They reascend the Mountain, while the Magician stands at his Cave Door, and sings, to encourage 'em. The Spirits, as before, present themselves in Opposition, but upon the Touch of the Wands, vanish upward and downward, with terrible Noises and Confusion. They gain the Summit of the Hill and entring the Enchanted Arches, strike the Gate with their Wands; when immediately the Palace, the Spirits, and the whole Mountain vanish away, and Godfrey and Eustatio are discover'd hanging on the sides of a vast Rock in the middle of the Sea; with much Difficulty they reach the Top, and descend on the other side.

After another scene in the enchanted garden, during which Armida and Rinaldo engage in hand-to-hand combat with supernatural reinforcements joining in on either side, there is a more orthodox but equally spectacular battle outside the walls of Jerusalem. Argante makes a reconnaissance attended by three generals—presumably his corps commanders. Both parties, accompanied by military music, hold a review of their entire forces, who salute as they march past. Each commander-in-chief draws up his army in order of battle and delivers a suitable harangue. At last, with a great blaze of trumpets and drums, "the Armies attack each other and form a regular Battle, which hangs in Balance, till Rinaldo having Storm'd the City, descends the Mountain with his Squadron, and assaults the Pagans in the Rear, who immediately fly, and are pursued by Rinaldo."

Similar effects occur in other operas of this period. The advertisements of *Teseo* mention "4 New Scenes . . . Decorations, Flights, and

Machines." The most elaborate scene is the last, in which Medea enters "in a Chariot drawn by flying Dragons," the palace catches fire, the sky is darkened by a thunderstorm, and Minerva descends from heaven in a machine. The machines in *Amadigi* were so numerous that the custom of allowing privileged listeners to sit on the stage was suspended in order to leave room for the operators. One of the attractions in this opera was a fountain, described with perhaps unconscious irony as "the Fountain of True Love" because it showed a lover what his beloved was doing in his absence. Even *Silla*, composed for the Earl of Burlington's private theater and not a magic opera,[5] has a scene that seems to demand extraordinary exertions from stagehands and singers alike. It shows a sea coast by moonlight with a small vessel and a boat on the beach. Silla embarks in the vessel, which sails away; but it is soon wrecked in a storm, during which a large comet appears. Silla dives overboard and swims to a rock; his wife Metella, who has been seeing him off, resolutely enters the boat, rows it out to the rock, snatches Silla, and carries him away.

In these early works Handel did not always match the action with suitable music (or if he did it has not survived). Act III of *Rinaldo* contains two battle symphonies and two marches, but the magic episodes, unlike the military, are not integrated by musical means. The score carries no suggestion of the supernatural, which, together with the terrible and amazing noises, is left to the imagination and the stagehands. This is not true of later operas. The music for the Furies in *Admeto* and for the various magic effects in *Orlando* is of superlative quality and a functional element in the drama, which it lifts to an altogether higher level.

The introduction of magic has another important result; it alters the whole ambience of the opera. We may take the cynical point that where the characters and landscape are no longer subject to ordinary criteria of behavior, the improbabilities of opera seria are less likely to bother an audience. Unto the magician all things are possible, so why worry if the plot appears inconsequent? But there is more to it than this. The miraculous can release the imagination of the composer as

[5] There is one supernatural episode; see p. 171 below.

well as of the audience, and open the way to fantasy and romanticism. In Handel this leads to a more complex scheme of motives and values. The elements that Metastasio was so careful to purge—the supernatural, the spectacle, the dilution of the tragic with the comic and the heroic with the vernacular—not only inspired some of Handel's greatest music; they are qualities intimately associated with romanticism in art. This is most conspicuous in the early nineteenth century, but is by no means confined to that period. Metastasio was a classical master in the strict sense, who built his aesthetic on reason and exalted it to the point where it became inhuman. Handel's genius, while comprehending the classical virtues, that of dramatic detachment in particular, contained a romantic streak as well.

This appears from time to time in the heroic operas, especially the later ones, whose librettos go back beyond Metastasio, often as far as the seventeenth century. In *Silla*, in *Arianna*, and twice in *Giustino* the hero goes to sleep on stage and is gratified by some god with a vision of the future or a summons to special duty. On each occasion we find in close conjunction a nocturne (usually with some degree of scene-painting in the orchestra), a visible manifestation of the supernatural, and a modification—sometimes a positive upheaval—of the opera seria closed forms. Nocturnal scenes with a romantic flavor occur throughout Handel's work: in the heroic *Floridante*, *Ottone*, and *Rodelinda;* in the antiheroic *Flavio;* in *Ariodante;* and in several of the oratorios, notably *Saul* and *Theodora.* They are a special characteristic of the magic operas. It is surprising too how often the favorite devices of nineteenth-century romantic opera are anticipated. Some of Handel's later operas employ choruses of sailors, soldiers, huntsmen, and so on almost as vehicles for local color in the manner of Weber or Auber, as well as descriptive instrumental passages. In *Giustino* the hero, a man of the people (who of course turns out to have noble blood), rescues one princess from a bear and another from a sea-monster in full view of the audience. One of the characters in *Amadigi* returns very impressively after death as a ghost, and *Rinaldo*, like *Oberon*, has a scene for two mermaids. These exotic episodes would have no particular significance if they did not regularly inspire Handel to some exceptional felicity and unorthodoxy in the music.

The scores bear eloquent witness to the appeal of this kind of subject. The early magic operas are wonderfully rich in invention, more so than the heroic works of the same period, and all five show striking features in the characterization. In four of them the hero is placed between two women, the sorceress who loves him and means to get him (and sometimes succeeds for a time) and the faithful but by no means spiritless spouse who wins him back. The sorceress is of course a perennial operatic type, whether she works by magic or (like Carmen or Manon or Lulu) by animal magnetism. In romantic opera the end is generally tragic, with the man and woman both destroyed. In Handel this cannot happen, but the climax is tragic in a different and perhaps more subtle way. The male victims escape the snare and pair off happily, as the convention requires; but it is the fate of the sorceress—the spider, not the fly—that moves Handel. In each of these operas he bestows his finest music on the creature who, despite the devilish use of her supernatural powers, cannot command the love of the mortal man she covets. To the librettist, and the audience, these may have been picturesque fairytales; Handel turns them into tragedies of disappointed love. Although three of them take their titles from the heroes, it is the sorceresses—Armida, Medea, Melissa, and Alcina—who capture our sympathy, and whose emotions we recognize (through the paradox of art) as the most human. Handel's music transcends the librettos; the magic element, designed perhaps as an excuse for diversion and the titillation of the senses, becomes a vehicle for profound truths about human nature. In the process it tells us much about Handel's personality as an artist and a man.

In *Rinaldo*, the least satisfactory of the group, Armida is the only character who comes to life. Despite her rather meager treatment by the librettist she emerges as a full-length preliminary study for Alcina. *Teseo* and *Amadigi* are based on French librettos, with the important choral scenes cut or replaced by episodes for minor characters. This produces an unbalanced design and a good deal that is obscure and absurd. *Amadigi* ends with a particularly feeble deus ex machina: the heroine's uncle, a magician by profession and a soprano, drops down unannounced to straighten out the plot, though he has made no effort to intervene while she was in mortal danger, and we have not heard of his existence. His prototype in Destouches's opera appears in the allegorical Prologue, which is cut in Handel's. In both operas, however, the sorceress dominates everything.

In *Teseo,* a hybrid between the classical-heroic and magic types, Handel was plainly inspired (like Cherubini later) by the towering figure of Medea; but her rival Agilea is movingly drawn, and Teseo himself has some exquisite music. Medea is a monster, with something of Agrippina and Armida in her make-up. Handel introduces her in a quiet and very beautiful arioso beginning with the "Comfort ye" fingerprint on the oboe (her first words are "Dolce riposo")—a clever touch, since the rest of her part is an epitome of bitterness, anger, jealousy, and despair. Twice she ends an act with an impassioned accompanied recitative leading to an explosive aria; such scenes never fail to rouse the dramatic fire in Handel. In Act IV she invokes the Furies in a strange aria with the voice, doubled by the violins, supplying the bass and the oboes in two parts above. The rhythm alone is enough to put the Furies in our mind, since Handel was to repeat the association in *Orlando* and Gluck in *Orfeo.* The magnificent scene in the last act in which Medea, no longer able to bear the happiness of the lovers, resolves on vengeance and death, looks forward in the opening figure of its ritornello to the jealousy chorus in *Hercules* and in general design to Alcina's "Ah! mio cor." The first half is based on contrasted adagio and presto strains (example 14, pp. 84–85). It culminates in a substantial ritornello of twelve bars on a fresh development of the material. The gloating second half (Allegro), in common time and the relative major key, drops back in full career to her "Morirò" with an effect of utter desolation.[6] Her final appearance is no less striking, and again exploits the virtue of surprise. Entering in her dragon chariot, she declares that the lovers are not free from her rage since hell is armed on her behalf. Her arioso plunges abruptly into G minor fom a secco cadence in E minor, is interrupted by cries for help from the other characters, and leads via a menacing unison passage[7] (as she disappears) into the gracious and richly scored ritornello for the descent of Minerva in glory. Until this point the upper instruments have been silent throughout the scene (example 15, pp. 86–87).

[6] Compare ex. 4, p. 46 above.

[7] Handel was to use this again at the beginning of the mad scene in Act II of *Orlando.*

Example 14

Example 15

SCENA VI.

MEDEA sopra un carro tirato da dragoni che volano, e detti.

SCENA VII.

Partita MEDEA, restano i medesimi personaggi in scena, e doppo sopragiunge MINERVA in gloria sopra una macchina.

Sortita MINERVA, cantando il seguente Recitativo accompagnato da una Sinfonia di stromenti.

The libretto of *Amadigi* is so badly botched that it is surprising Handel could make anything of it at all. Apart from Oriana's uncle, who is restricted to a few bars of recitative, it has only four characters, all sopranos or altos, two of whom are dead before the end. Handel must have had extra singers for the coro. Neither the structural nor the tonal balance is secure. Many of the ritornellos run to enormous length, and Act I in particular suffers from monotony of rhythm, tex-

Example 16

ture, and tonality; eight of its eleven arias are in B flat or G minor, and most of them in triple time. Four times in the opera (twice in succession in the second act) we find two consecutive arias in the same key, a situation avoided in the mature operas. Yet the subject made an evident appeal to Handel. The score is full of surprises, and remarkable for its romantic tinge. The secco recitative is exceptionally bold in its harmonic range, for example in the first scene of Act II, where the distraught Amadigi, horrified by a vision of his faithful Oriana courting another man, faints in the middle of a word (example 16).

Dardano's three solos in the second and third acts, the last of them as a ghost, are all strikingly original. Amadigi, except in the slow arias where he is suffering emotional torture, is a somewhat narcissistic hero. But Melissa, the sorceress whose spells spin the plot and who commits suicide when he deserts her, is more moving than Armida or Medea because she is so much more human. For all her evil deeds, she is a tragic figure destroyed by passion, and her fate darkens the last act—the earliest instance in Handel of an opera ending in a minor key. Her final utterance, like Medea's, is an arioso, but its impact is very different. The simplicity of its Sarabande rhythm provides a wonderful contrast with her earlier Medea-like outbursts; its single ritornello comes at the end, like a dirge, after she is dead (example 17, p. 90).

The last two magic operas, *Orlando* and *Alcina*, composed in Handel's maturity nearly twenty years later, are both masterpieces—thanks to their librettos (which come from the same source, Ariosto's epic *Orlando Furioso*) as well as their music. The supernatural and spectacular episodes never interfere with the basic human situations, as they sometimes do in *Amadigi;* the parts are subordinate to the whole. Each opera boasts a magnificent trio that draws the action together (though not at the same point) and a conclusion that satisfies every artistic demand. No more need be said of *Alcina*. *Orlando* differs from the rest of the group in that the supernatural agent, the magician Zoroastro, is male, not female. But the central theme is once more the suffering inflicted by love—it could be summed up in a line from Orlando's mad scene, "Since, even in Erebus, Love calls out Tears"—and the conflict is all on the human level.

There are four characters besides Zoroastro. Angelica and Medoro,

Example 17

an African prince, enjoy a mutual devotion, but each is loved vainly
by another: Angelica by the paladin Orlando, Medoro by the shepherdess
Dorinda. Orlando has saved Angelica's life; she admits that she is faithless
to him, but how can she help loving Medoro? The opera contrasts the
violence of Orlando's passion, which drives him over the brink of insanity, with the equally fruitless love of Dorinda, who can observe her
own feelings with a certain ironical detachment, and both with the
happiness of Angelica and Medoro. In the words of the Argument to
the printed libretto, the story "tends to demonstrate the imperious
Manner in which Love insinuates its Impressions into the Hearts of
Persons of all Ranks; and likewise how a wise Man should be ever ready
with his best Endeavours to re-conduct into the Right Way, those who
have been misguided from it by the Illusion of their Passions."

Handel, as we might expect, gives more reality to this "Illusion"
than to the moral it is supposed to enforce. While he wins our sympathy
for all the characters, Orlando, the victim of frustrated love, inspires
some of the most heart-searching music he ever wrote. The libretto may
seem complex and in places absurd; but it is transfigured in performance,
since its situations are psychologically and universally true and can carry
a profound symbolic content. In this and other respects, including the
vague African background, there is a kinship with *The Magic Flute*.
Both operas have a similar theme in the trials of a heroic lover, and the
magician who imposes them and pulls the strings is one and the same;
Sarastro is of course a variant of the name Zoroastro. It is even possible to
detect musical parallels, for Handel wrote the part of Zoroastro for
Montagnana, who had a compass of two octaves down to bottom F and
was renowned for his performance of cantabile arias with wide leaps in
the melody.

Nor does Handel suffer by this comparison. Musically *Orlando* is
perhaps the richest of all his operas. It is also the one in which he most
frequently breaks the bonds of opera seria by incorporating action,
sometimes of extreme violence, within the confines of the aria or duet
and modifying the form radically as a result. Besides the trio there are
three duets, none of which runs a regular course, musically or dramatically. In Act I Angelica, thinking herself alone, puts her love for
Medoro into words; Medoro overhears her and replies ardently in the

Example 18

Example 19

relative minor. According to the libretto Angelica should repeat her words in a da capo, or we might expect the whole piece to be a da capo love duet; but Handel continues straight on in recitative, leaving a free arioso that never regains its tonic and in which the characters sing in turn but never together.

The two duets in Act III are more eccentric; their form reflects the insanity that has warped Orlando's mind and turned him temporarily into a fiend. In the first he addresses Dorinda as Venus and to her astonishment makes passionate love to her. The music is restless in tonality and tempo, oscillates at irregular intervals between triple and common time, and again runs on into recitative without the voices singing together (example 18, pp. 92–93).

Later Orlando meets Angelica and mistakes her for a faithless mistress. She mourns Medoro, whom she believes Orlando has killed; Orlando says he wants her blood, not her tears. This duet is carefully built up in terms of dynamics, accompaniment, and length of phrase. In Angelica's solos the bass plays pianissimo without harpsichord or bassoons; these instruments enter forte when Orlando sings. The solos of each grow shorter and shorter, till at the climax both voices are briefly and for the first time heard together. Then (to quote the stage directions) he "seizes her by Force" and "throws her furiously into the Cave." Needless to say, there is no da capo.

The arias have an equal flexibility, and so do the accompanied recitatives, which are more numerous than in any Handel opera except

Tamerlano. The most striking example of both is the astonishing finale of Act II, in which Orlando's madness declares itself for the first time. Driven into a frenzy of jealousy by a love scene between Angelica and Medoro, he imagines he sees Charon's boat on the banks of the Styx, Pluto with his head surrounded by smoke and flames, Cerberus barking, and Medoro lying in Proserpine's arms. When he tries to attack Medoro, Proserpine's weeping makes him hesitate, but he hardens his heart and declares that nothing can ever calm his fury. This almost Freudian vision is set by Handel in a series of linked accompanied recitatives, some of them virtually ariosos, followed by a rondo whose episodes are so sharply contrasted that they threaten to tear the music apart. The scene runs to some two hundred bars, with nine changes of time signature and several tempo marks. Among its peculiarities is the earliest recorded use of quintuple time, which Burney thought would have been intolerable in any sane context. Handel introduces it with characteristic lack of symmetry, three bars at a time and one more a little later. The Cerberus passage with its distinctive rhythm and stern octaves must have been in Gluck's mind when he composed Act II of *Orfeo*. The first episode of the rondo, on a chromatic ground, seems to explore the depths of human suffering (example 19, pp. 94–95). The second episode modulates stormily in a rapid quaver and semiquaver motion, ending in A minor, after which the suave F major Gavotte melody (chosen perhaps for its ironic implications)[8] makes a breathtaking return. The climax comes in the orchestral coda, where the rondo theme appears for the last time as the cave into which Orlando has rushed, hoping to kill Medoro, "bursts open, and discovers the Magician seated in his Car, who clasps Orlando in his Arms, and flies thro' the Air."

The later stages of the last act show the other side of the picture, the serenity that succeeds to madness.[9] Orlando declares in accompanied recitative that he has purged the world of monsters and, exhausted by his struggles and sufferings, falls asleep. Zoroastro decides that the hour

[8] Handel uses the same marking, *A tempo di Gavotta*, for Orlando's mad aria in Act III, "Già lo stringo." See p. 161 and example 31 below.

[9] There is one further alarm, which produces the most telling dramatic stroke of all, when Angelica prevents Orlando from committing suicide—in the middle of an aria. See example 32, p. 170 below.

of rescue is at hand. Invoking the ruling spirit of the universe to send down a cure for Orlando's "Love-distemper'd Soul," he "makes a Signal with his Wand, and four Genij in the Air accompany an Eagle, who descends with a golden Vessel in his Beak. Zoroaster receives it, and then the Eagle and the Genij fly through the Air." Orlando's aria, scored for two solo viole d'amore and pizzicato basses and again without a da capo, is one of the most beautiful of the many sleep arias scattered through the operas. They all have a rapt haunting quality, as if sleep were to Handel an aspect of the supernatural. This is accentuated by Zoroastro's B flat minor recitative and the exquisite music (pianissimo strings without harpsichord) for the eagle and genii that follows. Music, drama, and spectacle are perfectly balanced, and the romantic accent is once more unmistakable. Zoroastro indeed seems to point not so much to *The Magic Flute* as to Wotan and Valhalla (example 20, pp. 98–99).

Example 20

Fà segno colla verga, e quattro genj per aria accompagnano un'aquila che porta un vaso d'oro becco. ZOROASTRO prende il vaso, e l'aquila con li genj vola via per aria.

Violini.

Viola.

Bassi.

Il mago s'accosta ad Orlando, quando esce Dorinda.

CHAPTER 7

✤✤✤✤✤✤✤✤✤✤✤✤

Antiheroic Operas

A modern listener is easily puzzled by the tone of Handel's librettos, and in particular by doubt as to how seriously they ought to be taken. Having heard them described as lofty and heroic, he may find it difficult not to laugh in the wrong place, or what he suspects is the wrong place. He deserves sympathy. The whole convention is apt to seem absurd today; and it is all too easy in a stage performance to turn serious scenes into farce or ironical episodes into empty heroics. But it would be wrong to regard every opera seria libretto as equally heroic in intention, though the characters are kings and queens and the subject matter the usual conflict between love and affairs of state. There may be fine distinctions between the matter of the plot and the temper in which the authors approach it. The eighteenth century knew enough about the seamier side of court life, and artists were capable of having a sly dig at corruption in high places, especially when they could do so under the guise of portraying the rulers of the remote or classical past. Some librettos undoubtedly contain satirical shafts intended for contemporary ears which ours can no longer pick up.[1] Not that Handel or his collaborators made fun of the Hanoverian dynasty—the only clear references to it, in *Riccardo Primo* and *Atalanta*, are loyal to the point of flattery—but they did not intend all the royal persons presented to be viewed with equal

---

[1] Michael F. Robinson (*Opera before Mozart,* London, 1966, p. 77) quotes an example from Vienna in 1674, where the identifications have been preserved by chance thanks to manuscript notes in a copy of the libretto.

solemnity. Some of their foibles are treated with unconcealed mockery. So on occasion are the operatic conventions themselves.

It is particularly difficult to judge the tone, and all the more important to do so correctly, when heroic, comic, and satirical elements are combined in the same libretto. This is by no means rare in Handel's operas; the most heroic contain touches of irony that relax the rigid posture of the characters and deepen their humanity,[2] and the supernatural, as we have seen, is not confined to the magic operas. Handel seems to have taken special pleasure in these mixed types, perhaps because they broaden the scope of the characterization. One of the most rewarding features of his dramatic works (including the oratorios) is the adoption of what appear to be antithetical approaches—the heroic and the antiheroic, the ironic and the pathetic, the romantic and the farcical—not only in the same work but in the same dramatic situation. And like Mozart, Handel is absolutely surefooted in moving from one plane to another and back. He had a rich gift of humor, but he never let it out of hand, a point his modern interpreters need to bear in mind. Insofar as the libretto allowed, he remained in sympathy with his characters and a detached observer of their destiny.

I have given the title "antiheroic" to those librettos that contain a prominent element of mockery, parody, or satire. I use the term only for convenience, and for want of a better. Handel certainly did not think of his operas by categories; he approached each libretto in the spirit it seemed to demand and, being a multifarious artist, refused to be confined by any stereotyped tone or method. All the categories overlap. The antiheroic operas include serious, romantic, or heroic themes and characters, so that both sides of the medal are on view at once. Their mood is more relaxed than that of the heroic operas, but it can be drawn taut as the situation requires. Their fascination lies precisely in this inclusiveness; they present life in its tragic and comic aspects, as an experience that comprehends both, but an artistically unified experience. This element in Handel has received little attention. Eisenschmidt asserts that Handel regarded comedy and parody as hostile to dramatic illusion,

[2] For example Asteria's teasing aria "Non è più tempo" in Act II of *Tamerlano*.

and although he finds comic touches in some librettos he suggests that Handel missed the point and took them seriously. It is Eisenschmidt who misses the point: in his discussion of the question he ignores the two operas in which parody is most subtly pervasive, *Flavio* and *Partenope*, ranking them tacitly with the heroic class.

Before considering the antiheroic operas in detail it is necessary to mention three works that fall into no category. Two of them, *Il Pastor Fido* and *Atalanta*, belong to the same pastoral convention as the English masque *Acis and Galatea*, though they have more contrived happy ends. The scene is a mythical Arcadia, the characters are, or pretend to be, shepherds and shepherdesses (the context is so artificial that the difference is immaterial), and their sole interests are love and hunting. *Atalanta*, an occasional piece written to celebrate the wedding of the Prince of Wales in 1736, ends with a sort of apotheosis, a suite of choruses and instrumental symphonies in the manner of Rameau. The chorus, which has been playing the part of Arcadian shepherds and shepherdesses, comes forward and declares that the marriage has assured the future of the dynasty, since no vile issue can spring from such a union. (What did spring from it was George III.) At the climax the orchestra is reinforced by three trumpets and drums and a display of fireworks. According to the libretto "the Scene opens and discovers Illuminations and Bonfires, accompanied by loud Instrumental Musick." Perhaps the chief matter for surprise is that Covent Garden had to wait seventy-two years to be burned down.

A more important opera is *Ariodante*, whose plot, like those of *Orlando* and *Alcina*, comes from Ariosto. It contains a good deal of pageantry, including a tournament in the lists and some big scenes for ballet and chorus, with a windband on the stage in the last act. But unlike the other operas based on Renaissance epics it has no supernatural or magic content; and the temper is neither heroic, despite the rank of the characters, nor antiheroic. The emotional level is that of every-day human conduct. The libretto is almost unique for its period in having no subplot. Everything contributes to the central situation, a story of sexual jealousy that might occur in any place, time, or rank of society.

Ariodante is about to marry Ginevra, daughter of the King of Scotland, with her father's blessing. Polinesso, Duke of Albany, also loves Ginevra, and is himself loved by her lady-in-waiting Dalinda. On the night before the wedding he persuades Dalinda to dress up in Ginevra's clothes and arranges for her to admit him into Ginevra's bedroom, watched by Ariodante from the garden. Ariodante, convinced that he has been betrayed, leaves the court in despair. Polinesso discards Dalinda and tries to have her murdered to keep her mouth shut. But Ariodante drives off the murderers, learns the truth, and kills Polinesso in the lists, thereby saving the life of Ginevra, who has been condemned to death by her father for unchastity. Shakespeare used the central episode in *Much Ado About Nothing*, and the story became a great favorite in the early romantic period, with operatic settings by Méhul, Berton, Mayr, and others within a few years. Weber's *Euryanthe* is a variant of it, and this in turn was one of the models for *Lohengrin*. It is easy to see why this mixture of realism and romanticism appealed equally to the early nineteenth century and to Handel. It is worth noting too how many of his best librettos are based on good literary sources. At least two of his operas, *Rodelinda* and *Flavio*, and three of his oratorios go back to Corneille or Racine. Ariosto provided three more. His blend of humanism, romanticism, and irony—the spiritual antithesis of Metastasio—must have been very congenial to Handel.

The score of *Ariodante* confirms this. It also reflects Handel's intense love for the countryside, which goes far beyond the demands of the pastoral convention and emerges most clearly in his setting of Milton's *L'Allegro* and *Il Penseroso* and in late oratorios like *Solomon* and *Susanna*. Many of his operas contain garden or woodland scenes, often at night, and they are quite different in atmosphere from his interiors. In *Ariodante* more than half the action takes place in the open air. The second act begins with a little ten-bar sinfonia (example 21, p. 104) depicting night and the rising of the moon over the palace garden. It is an incomparable piece of tone-painting and a vivid stroke of dramatic irony: with Polinesso on the stage, it prepares the background for the cruel deception of Ariodante by the false Ginevra. The moonrise was introduced by Handel; it is not in the source libretto.

As in *Orlando*, Handel varies the traditional forms with particular skill in the duets, of which there are four, only one with a regular da capo. The first is exquisitely placed in the second scene of the opera.

Example 21

SINFONIA.

Ariodante, alone in the garden, sings of his love in an arioso of haunting
beauty, richly accompanied by oboes and five-part strings (three violins).
Ginevra appears, and he tells her in recitative that he is too humble to
ask for her hand. In a touching phrase, without preliminary ritornello,
she offers it to him ("Prendi da questa mano"). This is the start of the

duet, but the fact is concealed till eight bars later, when Ariodante enters in the dominant and takes her hand ("Prendo"). After a regular second part Handel inserts a little two-bar ritornello to introduce the da capo. But now there are two surprises. Ariodante, confident of Ginevra's love, answers her after one bar instead of eight; and two bars later the duet is broken off by the King, her father, who comes in behind, takes both their hands, and gives them his blessing in recitative, the action continuing without a break (example 22).

The whole scene is a miracle of art, achieved by the simplest means. This is the first time we meet any of the characters except Ginevra; yet by the end we know all about their relationship. There are no da capos and therefore no exits. Everything builds up to the King's interruption, which coming just as we reach the expected da capo achieves the maximum surprise; and it conveys movingly and economically the dramatic

Example 22

point that he favors the union of the lovers. The librettist, Salvi, gave Handel a fine opportunity;[3] he seized and consolidated it in terms of music, especially (as on so many occasions) by subtle spacing of the ritornellos and vocal entries.

The second duet for Ginevra and Ariodante, at the end of the first act, runs into a chorus and ballet on the same material. The duet for Dalinda and Ariodante's brother Lurcanio in Act III is unique in at least two particulars. It is the only duet in Handel's London operas in which a tenor takes part, and like "Prendi da questo mano," but in a different way, it carries the action forward by means of a design that matches the situation with great psychological insight. Hitherto Dalinda, infatuated with Polinesso, has refused to look at Lurcanio. Her eyes have been opened to the fact that Polinesso has been using her for his own purposes, but she is inhibited by shame. In this long duet Lurcanio gently woos and wins her. It begins like a tenor aria; not till the thirty-seventh bar does Dalinda respond and sing for the first time.

All the music for Ariodante, Ginevra, and the King is of first-rate quality; if Polinesso and Dalinda had been more strongly drawn, especially in the earlier scenes, *Ariodante* would rank among Handel's greatest operas. Other features of this score, notably its organic employment of the ballet, will be considered later.[4]

Handel's antiheroic operas are scattered over his whole career and include his first venture in the form, *Almira*, and his last three. He was nineteen when he composed *Almira*, and it would be too much to expect him to manage the abrupt swings in mood and temper with assurance. The comic element is supplied by the servant Tabarco, who like Elviro in *Serse* (the only other character in Handel's operas belonging to the buffo tradition, or more strictly to its antecedent, the comic intermezzo) enjoys himself by mocking the love-sick plight of his masters. In Act I, after a passionate misunderstanding between two lovers, Tabarco opens one of the lady's love-letters which he has been sent to post, shakes his head solemnly over it, and ends the act with a lively parody of his social superiors. The first scene of Act III is a spectacular charade influenced

---

[3] The arioso and the interrupted duet are in the original, but Handel shortened the dialogue between them.

[4] See pp. 142–143 below.

by the French opera-ballet. The queen and the court ladies sit in galleries, with their bodyguard and household ranged below, while three fancy-dress processions enter, each led by a character representing one of the continents with a train of dancers, instrumentalists, and attendants in costumes appropriate to the various nations. First Europe in a horse-drawn wagon, wearing Roman habit with crown, orb, and scepter, preceded by a band of oboes; then Africa under a canopy borne by twelve Moors, with trumpets and kettledrums; then Asia in oriental costume, pulled by lions and carrying quivers and arrows, led by cymbals, side-drums, and fifes. Last comes an antimasque (not, it would seem, intended to represent America): Tabarco rides in on horseback dressed as Folly, with a lyre and bagpipes and a train of harlequins and other comedians. While everyone argues over which continent should have the prize, he claims the greater part of the human race as his subjects.

The music is not distinguished, though the possibility that the various instruments mentioned in the stage directions took part in the eight songs and dances, which with one exception are scored for a tutti treble line and bass, is intriguing, and the Sarabande of the Asiatics was to become famous as the aria "Lascia ch'io pianga" in *Rinaldo*. But the episode is worth mentioning since it shows that Handel, like other baroque opera composers, was dealing with a very mixed form. The Italian strain in his music is still second-hand, weaker and clumsier than the German and French. The dance rhythms, in the arias as well as the ballets, are mostly Gigues and Sarabandes; the Sicilianos, which he learned from Scarlatti and was to exploit with such wonderful resource for the rest of his life, lay in the future.

Agrippina, composed five years later, reveals a far more confident touch, as well as the fertilizing influence of Italy. The libretto has a strong flavor of irony and the same equivocal moral tone we find in Monteverdi's *Coronation of Poppea*. The one consistently serious character is Ottone, who attains tragic stature. The others, including the entire imperial family, are morally contemptible; but the result is not repulsive or dramatically fatal, as in some of Metastasio's librettos, because they are never represented—and do not represent themselves—as anything else. Claudio, the Emperor, is a pompous ass with a foretaste of the elderly and amorous basses of Rossini and Donizetti. The trio in which he is whisked out of Poppea's bedroom by Poppea herself and his servant Lesbo (another bass) before his wife can catch him is a pure buffo situation, though its musical exploitation is not developed. There is a humorous quartet in which Agrippina and her two freedmen, by prearrangement, salute Nero as Emperor and he is graciously pleased to accept. Handel set this as a free arioso almost in Monteverdi's manner, ending with a solo for Nero. Its most striking feature is the progressive tonality: it begins in A minor with the offer, and ends in C major with its acceptance.[5] The fact that the whole thing is a put-up job adds an edge to the wit. Familiar too from later comic opera is the delight of all the characters (except Ottone) in intrigue for its own sake. This is very different from the heavy-handed and contrived intrigues of the heroic operas, and is treated with such a light touch that we accept it with pleasure. Up to a point the librettist, who was a cardinal, was poking fun at the heroic convention.

But he was at the same time accepting it, and so was Handel. A modern director must draw the line between laughing with the authors and laughing at them. There is little comedy in the arias. One or two of Claudio's come close to parody, but they deserve a smile rather than a belly laugh. The libretto and the music make it plain that the emotions of the characters are genuine, and that Agrippina, for instance, is a woman to be reckoned with. The recitative is more equivocal. Many of the situations are very funny. The two toadying freedmen who offer to do Agrippina's dirty work in the hope of being rewarded with her love, which she has no intention of giving them, and who always enter one after the other, cannot be taken with a straight face. The bedroom scene in Act III, with three of Poppea's suitors distributed behind screens in helpless indignation, seems made for Rossini; and Claudio's ultimate dismissal of Poppea (after chasing her around for three acts) as more trouble than she is worth is a delicious anticlimax. Nor need Poppea's professions of purity be taken seriously. But to turn all this into buffoonery is to risk queering the pitch for the next aria. A balance can be struck that preserves the passionate and pathetic aspect of the characters

[5] This plan is a refinement introduced by Handel. In the printed libretto of 1709 the quartet ends with a repeat of Agrippina's salutation.

without losing a sense of the ludicrous. As in Mozart's operas, it is a matter of finding the style of high comedy—comedy, not farce.

Poppea is fond of Ottone, and his love for her is an all-consuming passion, like that of Monteverdi's Nerone. The second-act garden scene in which Poppea, after publicly snubbing Ottone, pretends to go to sleep in order to hear him declare his love anew may have been meant as a parody of the conventional sleep scene; Handel's music makes it much more. It becomes a clever revelation of character, responding to every shade of mood; it is also a masterly manipulation of form. Ottone's aria "Vaghe fonti," beautifully scored for recorders, muted violins, and pizzicato basses (at first without harpsichord), evokes the open-air setting and the singer's feelings with the utmost eloquence. He breaks off into secco recitative when he sees Poppea. The arioso that follows in an unexpected key (G minor after F major) is the second part, but it is several times interrupted by Poppea calling out as if in a dream and finally by her pretending to wake up. Handel keeps us in suspense for the da capo that never comes. Instead Ottone sings another aria, "Ti vo' giusta," whose chromatic detail faintly anticipates "He was despised." The emotional link is clear.[6]

One of the most memorable features of this opera, again prophetic of later things, is the skill with which Handel delineates the two women, the ruthless, scheming Agrippina and the pliantly seductive Poppea. Some of Agrippina's music, especially the aria "Pensieri, voi mi tormentate" with its astonishing exposure of mental anguish and its contrasts in texture and mood (extreme even for Handel), has intense grandeur and passion. Agrippina, planning by foul means to obtain the throne for Nero, struggles with unuttered thoughts. The libretto leaves their nature in doubt; the music suggests a mixture of fear and guilt, all the more powerful because unrecognized. The opening, not unlike that of Medea's "Morirò" (example 14, p. 84), packs a world of emotion into very few notes (example 23, pp. 110–111). The first part spreads the same four words over forty-eight slow bars. The second part, contrasted in tempo,[7] rhythm (4/4), and scoring (four-

---

[6] See p. 69 and example 12 (p. 72) above.

[7] There are no tempo marks in the score, but the change is implicit in the music.

Example 23

SCENA XIII.

part texture), is a prayer to the gods for aid. Handel made important
changes in the words, giving them a more concrete definition.[8] The
da capo is foreshortened by the omission of the ritornello. But there is
another surprise in store. Agrippina continues (in secco recitative) to
ponder her nefarious plans and is weighing the merits of her victims,
when the first part of the aria returns in condensed form, like an obses-
sion she cannot shake off. A little later, having set her mind at rest by
making arrangements for three murders, she ends the act with a simile
aria, comparing herself to a steersman crowding on sail as he makes
for harbor. Handel's music, an irresistible prototype of a Viennese
waltz that must have started every foot in Venice tapping, suggests
the unscrupulous adventurer plunging with renewed zest into the fray.
There is somehow no discrepancy with what has gone before (example
24, p. 112).

[8] The printed libretto reads: "Numi eterni ch'il Ciel reggette,/ I miei voti rac-
cogliete,/ La mia spene secondate." Handel's "Ciel, soccorri" permits a much sharper
contrast with the first part.

Flavio is the one opera of the Royal Academy period that turns its back on the heroic style. The libretto, again Venetian in origin, is an odd but effective compound of Corneille's *Le Cid* and an episode in Dark Age Lombard history. Outwardly the double plot is the usual mixture of political and amorous intrigue; in temper it is an antiheroic

Example 24

(Violino I.)
(Oboe I.)
Tutti.
(Violino II)
(Oboe II.)

(Bassi.)

comedy with serious and at one point tragic undercurrents. Two elderly politicians, a tenor and a bass, are rivals for the vacant governorship of Britain; there may be some topical reference or private joke here.[9] The defeated candidate, Lotario, gives his successful rival, Ugone, a hearty smack across the cheek, which not only affronts his honor but leaves him with such a red face that he is ashamed to appear at court. Meanwhile the Emperor, Flavio, falls in love with Ugone's daughter Teodata, unaware that she loves his courtier and friend Vitige and is secretly living with him. When Flavio asks Vitige if he considers her beautiful, Vitige, hoping to put him off, says he does not. The Emperor thereupon orders him to procure her for him, and Vitige, not daring to disobey, tells Teodata to temporize, pretending to return Flavio's feelings. This she does, in the presence of Vitige, with such conviction that he cannot decide whether she is playing her part or really means it. He boils with jealousy but of course can say nothing, and Teodata, a girl of some spirit, adds to his discomfort by teasing him. The political plot takes a serious turn when Ugone's son Guido, burning to avenge his father's honor, which has been further mortified by the discovery that his daughter is living in sin with Vitige, kills Lotario in a duel. But the end of the opera is pure comedy, with Flavio—an emperor whose easy principles are seasoned with a sense of humor—laughing at the other characters and at himself. His last words, when the two plots have been unravelled, are: to Vitige "For punishment, give your unwilling hand to the woman you don't think beautiful," and to Ugone "He is worthy of your daughter, and now go off and govern Britain."

The tone of the libretto is so full of irony and even bathos (Vitige, after giving Teodata Flavio's message, says that if he does not get her back by sunset Ugone, Guido, Flavio, himself, and the whole world will perish by his sword) that it must have been meant as a parody of the whole opera seria convention. Handel characteristically gets the best of both worlds. There are several romantic, tragic, and highly emotional scenes: the nocturnal love duet for Vitige and Teodata with which the opera begins, the killing of Lotario on the stage, his daughter

[9] Since the reference to Britain occurs in Partenio's opera (Venice, 1682), on which Handel's libretto is based, it may have suggested the choice of subject in the first place.

Emilia's lament when she finds him dead, and Guido's despair when as a result of his act Emilia rejects his love. These last two arias in particular, Emilia's in F sharp minor, Guido's in B flat minor, are as emotionally profound as anything in Handel's grander operas. Elsewhere his touch is lighter, but full of musical resource. In its expression of emotional crosscurrents and its blend of comedy, irony, and pathos the score of *Flavio* shows an advance on *Agrippina* and looks forward to the unique individuality of *Serse* and *Imeneo*.

Partenope, seven years later than *Flavio*, has an even more hilarious climax—or rather anticlimax. Again the plot parodies the heroic style. Act I begins with a spectacular ceremony, the foundation of the city of Naples in mythical times by the young queen Partenope. She has three suitors, in hot competition for the post of consort. The one she prefers, Arsace, has deserted his betrothed Rosmira in order to woo Partenope. Rosmira however follows him from Greece to Naples disguised as a man, taxes him with his infidelity (which he cannot deny), and defies him to redeem his honor, if he can, by promising never in any circumstances to give away her identity. He consents, and she proceeds to taunt him before the whole court, finally challenging him to a duel. He of course tries to get out of this, with the result that he is derided as a coward by Partenope, the other suitors, and the disguised Rosmira herself. Partenope insists that the duel must take place in the lists before a court of chivalry. Arsace, still trying to wriggle out of it, is made to look more foolish than ever. But at the last moment he turns the tables: he *will* fight, on one condition: the duelists must be stripped to the waist. The tribunal agrees that this is within the rules, and Rosmira is exposed—in the figurative sense.

This scene, which is developed at considerable length and is very funny in the theater, is a send-up of the grand tournament scenes found in *Ariodante*, *Sosarme*, and other operas, including many written in the next hundred years. The same is probably true of the battle scenes in Act II, followed as they are by a ridiculous dispute among Partenope's suitors over which of them has contributed most to her victory. The plot makes sport of one of the most cherished opera seria conventions by placing the castrato hero in a succession of highly undignified situations all through the opera. It also exploits the popular device of sexual ambivalence, for Rosmira poses as a fourth suitor of Partenope. Thus a man, Arsace, is torn between love for a woman and an apparent man, Rosmira, and a woman disguised as a man pretends to be in love with another woman. Moreover one of the male suitors, Armindo, was played by a woman. Add the fact that Arsace, Armindo, and Rosmira are all mezzos or altos (Partenope is the one soprano), and we have a fruitful source of double meanings in which almost every aspect of the heroic opera can be mocked in turn. Metastasio would have been unspeakably shocked. The happy end turns out to be a satisfactory unraveling of the plot, since Partenope has been disillusioned by Arsace's shilly-shallying and accepts Armindo instead, thus releasing Arsace to return to Rosmira.

The score does not rank with Handel's finest, but it contains another ravishing sleep scene in Act III, and the arias, mostly light in texture, express the emotions of the characters with sympathy and tenderness. Handel makes fun of the situations, not the characters; his method is closer to Mozart's in *The Marriage of Figaro* than to Rossini's in *The Barber of Seville*. Act III of *Partenope*, like Act I of *Agrippina*, contains a trio and a quartet; no other Handel opera has both, and it may be that the comic spirit was responsible for their inclusion. While these pieces make their mark in both operas, if only by varying the texture, they are all short (three of them between 12 and 25 bars), and are not so placed as to draw the main threads of the plot together. Nor do the voices sing all at once; indeed the *Partenope* quartet nowhere has more than two in simultaneous action. That Handel could write a concerted piece to crown a dramatic climax is proved by the trios in *Tamerlano, Orlando, Alcina*, and *Imeneo*, and the magnificent quartet in *Radamisto*, not to mention even greater movements in the oratorios. But the opera seria convention did not encourage this. The *Radamisto* quartet was inserted for one revival and then cut.

After the failure of the heroic operas of 1736–1737 Handel closed his operatic career with three decidedly antiheroic comedies. By this time the style and dramatic structure of the music had undergone certain changes. We have noted the influence of the later Neapolitans, which Handel, always a great eclectic, assimilated without difficulty alongside his old idiom, and the more liberal use of choral and instrumental movements. These Neapolitan-type arias have a lighter frame-work and a homophonic rather than polyphonic idiom, based on busy repeated-chord accompaniment figures. The result sometimes suggests Arne. Three separate arias in Act I of *Giustino* prefigure Arne's most famous melody, "Rule, Britannia."[10] The deviation towards comedy and the more relaxed treatment of the conventions, while implicit in the librettos, may have represented a personal choice: the heroic opera seria was to persist on the continent for several decades.

In none of these three operas does the castrato get the girl. In *Serse* he is defeated by a travesti mezzo, in *Imeneo* by a bass—the only instance of this in Handel, and an unthinkable event in Senesino's day. In *Deidamia* he is not in love with the heroine, so that the end of the opera assumes an odd air of detachment. Deidamia is to marry Achilles, though she knows that he must leave at once for Troy and never return. But Achilles was played by a woman; the castrato is Ulysses, who as leading man shares the final duet with Deidamia, handing her over to Achilles like an uncle giving away his niece in marriage. The coro that follows and ends the opera supplies a wry moral: let the lovers enjoy themselves while they can—when they separate, each can easily pick up a new partner. The entire libretto has this disillusioned flavor, with copious irony at the expense of the Greek heroes and even more sexual innuendo than *Partenope*. Despite its promising situations and a few superb arias, *Deidamia* must be considered a failure. It was Handel's last opera, and much of the music is mechanical, as if he were losing interest after discovering in *Saul* the greater dramatic potentialities of oratorio.

With *Serse* and *Imeneo* however he might almost be said to have conquered a new world. Outwardly the plot of *Serse* preserves many features of the heroic opera—love, warfare, politics, and intrigue—but the tone of the dialogue is light, even chatty, and every situation has a comic and a serious aspect, both exploited to the full. Part of the credit belongs to Minato's old Venetian libretto of 1654. As in *Partenope* there is a resounding anticlimax in the last scene, where Serse (the Xerxes of Greek history) thinks he is about to marry Romilda, only

---

[10] "Un vostro sguardo," "Se parla nel mio cor," and "Vanne, sì."

to find that, through an ambiguity in his orders, she has married his brother and rival Arsamene, whom she loves. At the same time his double-dealing is publicly exposed by Amastre, whom he has promised to marry but deserted, unaware that she has been watching him all through the opera disguised as a soldier. Again the castrato is presented in a ridiculous light. But unlike Arsace Serse is a monarch whose word is law; he exiles Arsamene and later condemns him to death. As a formidable figure whom it is dangerous to provoke, but who is finally forced to beg for forgiveness, his closest parallel is the Count in *The Marriage of Figaro*.

The other six persons illustrate the range of Handel's characterization. Three are primarily comic, though in very different ways. Ariodate, Serse's commander-in-chief and father of Romilda and Atalanta, is a vain and pompous general whose wits are just capable of misconstruing Serse's orders and marrying Romilda to the wrong man. Atalanta, the perfect foil to her sister, is one of opera's immortal flirts; after the failure of her schemes to steal her sister's lover, whom she does not love, she sails cheerfully off in search of new prey. In Arsamene's servant Elviro Handel created a buffo bass in the tradition later ornamented by Leporello. He grumbles at being dragged round as an accessory to his master's love-assignations when he would rather go to sleep; and Handel uses him to parody several of the stock opera seria situations, such as the disguise scene and the vengeance aria. When masquerading as a flower-seller in Act II he quotes street cries that Handel picked up in London. Later he has a comic drinking-song when the storm that destroys Serse's bridge of boats terrifies him and he hastens to drown his sorrows in a more acceptable liquor than the Hellespont.

Romilda, Amastre, and Arsamene are the serious characters. All are in love in their own despite—martyrs to it, not least when they consider its object unworthy of them, which is Amastre's case throughout and that of the others when they believe momentarily that they have been betrayed. As usual with Handel's star-crossed lovers, their music is emotional, sympathetic, and shot through with intimations of tragedy. We may gain some idea of Handel's feeling for character in this opera by comparing the arias of the two sisters that end the first two acts. They are too long to quote in full, but the ritornellos are sketches in outline. Atalanta expounds the principles that guide her conduct ("Un cenno leggiadretto, Un riso vezzosetto, Un moto di pupille Può far inamorar").

Example 25

Romilda, after rejecting Serse's advances in Act II, declares that her love for the exiled Arsamene will never swerve. Handel can hardly have been inspired by the words—their literal meaning is "He who yields to the fury of unfavorable stars is no lover"—but he penetrates to the emotions implicit in Romilda's situation and gives her a great paean of a melody, twenty bars long, that immortalizes her as an operatic character. The effect is strengthened by the art with which he extends the tune and later divides it in varying proportions between the voice and the violins (example 26).

The formal design of *Serse* is freer and less predictable than that of any other Handel opera. Half the arias have no da capo. Some are

Example 26

interrupted by recitative; others are repeated or quoted later.[11] The first two acts contain scenes of some length in which convention goes by the board and the music responds as if by instinct to what is happening on the stage. In each case one theme—the ritornello of Romilda's offstage arioso with its cool recorders in Act I, Elviro's street-song in Act II (underpinned with delicious incongruity by a ground bass)— returns at intervals to bind the whole together. Once more the duets

[11] See p. 177 below.

are irregular in form and dramatic content. In Act II Serse has two, with Romilda and Amastre. In the first, an exquisite miniature of eighteen bars without ritornellos, Romilda, confronted with apparent proof that Arsamene is false, cannot deny her love for him. In the entire accompaniment Handel wrote precisely twenty-one notes, all on the bass line. This is followed by a brilliant bravura aria for Serse with strings and oboes, and this in turn by an intensely passionate accompanied recitative and aria in which Romilda's jealousy and resentment burst forth unrestrained. The aria begins without ritornello; there has been no secco recitative since before the duet.

In the second duet Serse and Amastre, both singing aside, complain of the pangs of jealousy; their voices do not come together till the last three bars before the brief coda. The situation is complex and ironical, since Amastre is sighing for Serse, while Serse, who takes Amastre for a man, is thinking of Romilda. When Romilda and Arsamene at last have their duet in Act III, things run far from smoothly. Although they are about to be married they do not know it, and they have a furious quarrel before going out in opposite directions. In the next scene, just before the wedding, Handel introduces a sly quotation from this duet into the recitative.

The plot may seem involved, but in the theater the various relationships and their overtones come instantly to life.[12] The supreme quality of *Serse*, which ranks among the masterpieces of operatic comedy, lies not merely in the vitality of the characters and the aptness of the forms but in the artistic unity that Handel creates out of so much variety. Act II in particular veers between farce, ironic comedy, and high tragedy, with Elviro's buffo drinking-song jostling some of the most passionate love music ever written, and Atalanta's wiles set beside the loneliness of the deserted Amastre, not to mention the spectacular frustration of Serse's attempt to bridge the Hellespont. The light structure of these late Handel operas is deceptive; they take the whole range of human nature for their province. There is no way of appreciating Handel's surefootedness in moving from one level to another and back except to hear the opera complete, if possible in the theater. It is this balance of

[12] The fatal results of judging Handel outside the theater have seldom been better illustrated than in some American reviews of the recent recording of *Serse*.

humor and heart-break, combined with endless subtlety in harmony, rhythm, and length of phrase, that recalls the Mozart of *Figaro* and *Così fan tutte*, though as we have seen the historical link is rather with Monteverdi's Venice.

Handel's next and penultimate opera, *Imeneo*, was a total failure, and was never revived between 1742 and 1960. It is the one work in the series omitted from Loewenberg's *Annals of Opera*.[13] Yet its individual flavor almost entitles it to rank as a minor masterpiece. It is the story of two men, sung by a castrato and a bass, in love with the same girl, Rosmene, who has been kidnapped by pirates. She loves Tirinto, the castrato, but the bass, Imeneo, rescues her from the pirates, and public opinion, voiced by her father, expects her to reward him with her hand. Torn in opposite directions, she pretends to be mad. Under this protective cover she makes her choice—Imeneo. There is no subplot (except that Rosmene's sister Clomiri is in love with Imeneo), no complicated intrigue, and no spectacle. A single set suffices for the whole opera, which was written for a small cast of limited capacity.

The first big climax is the trio in Act II. The two suitors plead with Rosmene, who has been left to make her own choice; she feels drawn to both for different reasons, but cannot reconcile the demands of love and her pledged word on the one hand, and gratitude and alleged duty on the other. The conflict remains unresolved. But the trio dramatizes it much as Mozart or Verdi might have done. The mad scene in Act III is a brilliant parody of this old operatic device and at the same time a revelation of the real emotional disturbance in Rosmene's heart. The accompanied recitative in particular, with its wild modulations and snatches of haunting melody, has an almost Hamlet-like ambiguity. To what extent are her protestations genuine or feigned, or a mixture of both? We are left in doubt. But Rosmene retains our sympathy, and so (surprisingly, if we read the libretto by itself) does the close of the opera. Imeneo is a cool fish, who does not scruple to blackmail the fathers of Athens to gain his desire. Rosmene puts duty before love, but the somber final coro in the minor leaves no doubt

---

[13] Second edition (Geneva, 1955).

where Handel's sympathies lie. At the Dublin revival in 1742 he underlined this by inserting the exquisite love duet "Per le porte del tor-
mento" from *Sosarme* before the coro, sung not by the bridal pair
Rosmene and Imeneo but by Rosmene and Tirinto as they part for the
last time. Tirinto, as the leading man (though the part was probably
sung by Mrs. Cibber), perhaps had to have the duet even if he lost
the prima donna; Handel turned this limitation—if it is such—into a
stroke of genius and achieved a climax of extraordinary beauty and
pathos. As in the greatest of the operas and oratorios he tells us far more
about human nature than we could ever guess from the libretto.

CHAPTER 8

֍֍֍֍֍֍֍֍֍֍֍֍

The Craftsman in the Theater

Before examining in more detail Handel's exploitation of the opera seria convention it is necessary to glance at certain features of the theater for which his operas were written, and at the manner in which they were staged. While it is recognized that this differed from modern practice, its influence on the musical structure seems never to have been investigated. This is a matter of radical importance for the understanding of Handel as artist and dramatic craftsman. Eisenschmidt collected much information on theatrical conditions; except in a general way he did not relate it to the music. He told us how Handel's operas were produced, but not how this controlled their form. Few musicologists or stage directors seem to have considered the subject, partly perhaps because Eisenschmidt's book came out early in the war in a small edition and is not easily obtained. There are also vital points with which it deals inadequately or not at all.

One of these is the use of the curtain. In the English theaters of Handel's day the curtain rose and fell once only in the course of the evening, at the start of the opera and at the end of the last act. Except on rare occasions there were no intermediate curtains, either between scenes or between acts, until about 1750 (ten years afer Handel had stopped writing operas), when the curtain began to be lowered in act-intervals.[1] The scenery in all theaters until the nineteenth century was changed in full view of the audience; that indeed was its purpose—not

---

[1] Richard Southern, *Changeable Scenery* (London, 1952), p. 170.

to create illusion, but to excite wonder and delight. Its principal components were pairs of panels (shutters or back flats) meeting in the center of the stage, and a series of wings in echelon on either side. All worked by sliding in grooves. When we read in the librettos that the scene opens to reveal Parnassus in *Giulio Cesare*, Alcestis lying dead in *Admeto*, or the bonfires in *Atalanta*, the back flats were simply withdrawn; there was no question of a curtain.

All scene changes could be executed very rapidly, a single machine in one motion removing the old wings and flats and substituting a new set. At the same time the stage lighting (which was supplied by candles, but with the aid of shields and transparencies admitted a considerable range of effects) could be modified by rotating machines in the wings and by raising and lowering the footlight ramp. Sulphur was thrown on the candles to produce a sudden increase of light. If necessary a change could begin while a singer was finishing an aria on the projecting apron that was a feature of all London theaters. For successive scenes in the same act a great deal of variation was possible in the size of the playing area: apart from the apron, the main stage could be made deeper or shallower according to which of the scenery grooves were used to close the prospect; or it could be left open as far as the backcloth, which stood some distance behind the farthest grooves; or the backcloth too could be withdrawn and the depth almost doubled by taking in a room behind the stage. On the earliest known plan of the King's Theatre (see frontispiece) this is labeled "Chambre servant à alonger le Théatre"; in Michael Novosielski's scale drawing of 1782[2] it appears as a tea room, with the entrance marked "Doorway to Tea Room occasionally open into Stage." The immense depth must have greatly enhanced the spectacular scenes.[3]

The area beyond and on either side of the backcloth was set apart

[2] In the Soane Museum, London; identified by F. H. W. Sheppard, *The Survey of London*, vols. XXIX and XXX (London, 1960). Eisenschmidt reproduces the drawing, but dates it *ca.* 1720.

[3] Some theaters were built with a recess at this point, evidently for the same purpose of deepening the playing area. The extension may have been used in Act III of *Rinaldo*, where the mountain is described as "rising from the Front of the Stage, to the utmost Height of the most backward Part of the Theatre." See p. 78 above. For fuller particulars of methods of scene-changing and lighting, see Eisenschmidt's detailed account.

for the operation of machines, whether on the ground or in the air. Additional scenery (cloud borders and groundrows) could be used to mask their movements.[4] The London theater in Handel's day had reached a high degree of technical sophistication; if he had composed a *Flying Dutchman*, its staging would have presented no insuperable difficulties. In *Rinaldo* and *Giustino* ships are required to approach or sail away with some of the characters on board. In Act II of *Poro* an army crosses a river by a practicable bridge, which is later destroyed by a troop of pioneers, who "cause it to be broken down at both Ends, where it joins to the two Shores; after that, throwing his Sword and Helmet into the River, [Gandarte] then casts himself into it, follow'd by the Pioneers." Some of the most elaborate sets—the mountain palace stormed by the Crusaders in *Rinaldo*, the nether regions penetrated by Hercules in *Admeto*, the palace in *Ariodante* with practicable staircases and perhaps a minstrels' gallery for the stage band—seem to have employed a mixture of built and cut-out scenery in several planes. The former, like the "scenes of relieve" in the masques of Inigo Jones, would be set up behind the farthest grooves, with the back flats closed. This was the one type of scenery that could not be changed in view of the audience.

The restricted use of the curtain and the quick scene-changing had an enormous influence on the design of the operas. They explain some superficially puzzling features; for example, the two or three final bars, generally for reduced orchestra, after the voices have sung the coro,[5] were almost certainly intended to bring down the curtain while the company bowed and, if they were on the apron, retired behind the proscenium. With the curtain rising after the overture it was possible to begin the opera with a tableau, the whole cast assembled on stage supported by an army of supers. The last act could be built up to a tableau for the curtain. But an intermediate act or scene, though it might begin with two or three characters coming on together, could not have the initial impact obtained from a crowded stage. And the almost

[4] The back flats could be divided horizontally into two pairs, and the upper pair withdrawn if necessary without the lower.

[5] These codas are found in all Handel's London operas except *Amadigi* and *Arianna*. The former certainly, and the latter possibly, ended with a ballet.

invariable conclusion of the intermediate acts with a solo aria, or more rarely a duet, is conditioned by the fact that there was no curtain to build up to. Whoever was on stage simply walked off. Nor was the modern blackout possible, since some of the stage lights were always burning, and so incidentally—in England, though not on the continent —were the house lights.

We thus find a characteristic scene structure exactly opposite to what we are used to in the operatic repertory from Mozart to Verdi, which derives not from opera seria but from opera buffa. There the typical scene begins with one or two characters and builds steadily up to a concerted movement, with or without chorus, concluding as often as not with a dramatic gesture, a crescendo, a stretto, and a grand asseveration of the tonic key as the curtain falls. The opera seria scene, on the other hand, is distinguished by a gradual tapering off as each character sings his aria and goes out, until no one is left.

It would be wrong to dismiss this as a primitive scheme incapable of artistic development. It did tend to throw the outward emphasis in a different place, on the beginning of a scene rather than the end, especially at the start of the opera. But this had certain advantages. By opening with a tableau the librettist could launch his story on an effective climax and prolong the scene to considerable length. If there are six characters on stage when the curtain rises, it will be some time before the exit arias are exhausted, and unnecessary to devise pretexts for bringing any of them back.

The same conditions of course applied to all composers, and they reacted in different ways. Handel, as his works show again and again, was a master at turning limitations, or what look like limitations, to profitable account. Since his genius was evolutionary rather than revolutionary, and since the opera seria convention in which he signally exercised it was for long consigned to oblivion and contempt, his achievements in this field have never been recognized. He was credited in his own day (by Mainwaring, for example) with a great improvement of stage technique. It is therefore no surprise to find him developing his own methods of furthering the advantages and making capital out of the disadvantages of the system; using musical means and practical innovations (such as raising the curtain at an unexpected moment) to increase and prolong the impetus of the first scene, and evolving a kind of dramatic counterpoint to work the tapering-off process of the exits against an increase of emotional tension.

The quick scene change offered opportunities of a different kind. The continuity of the action enabled the composer either to make a sharp musical contrast or, if he wished, to extend the mood across the visual break. Handel's means here was his control of tonality. Some of his operas, such as *Ariodante* and *Imeneo*, have a clear overall tonal plan, like *Saul* and Mozart's operas. Quite a few more (Grout lists some of them)[6] show a gravitation towards certain keys for the most important movements. This is partly, but not entirely, conditioned by the restricted range of the wind instruments—trumpets in D, horns in F, and so on—and by associations of key with certain moods or *Affekte*. Handel undoubtedly saw some of his characters in terms of a prevailing tonality: Cleopatra (as first sung, though not in the original conception) in the bright keys of E and A major, Amarilli in *Pastor Fido* in G major and minor, Antigona in *Admeto* in B flat (she has four arias in that key).

Apart from these broad architectural schemes, all Handel's operas, even the earliest, have a carefully shaped internal plan, linked with scene changes, entry of characters, and the general progress of the drama. Where there is no change of scene the arias follow a recitative cadence in a related key except where the action demands an abrupt gesture of contrast.[7] This sequence is never left to chance: where it seems inconsequent in the printed scores, it is the scores that are wrong.[8] The harmonic progression is not always the same. Handel may jump into an aria from the dominant; the relative major or minor; the mediant, generally minor (a special favorite in his maturity); more rarely the subdominant, major or minor; and occasionally the tonic. He may begin an aria on an inversion of the tonic chord, or with a chord that suggests another key altogether, as in "Mirerò quel vago" in *Radamisto*. The important thing is that, like Beethoven in his instrumental works, he

[6] *A Short History of Opera* (1947), p. 172.

[7] For examples of this see pp. 83 above and 164 below.

[8] For instance, in Act I of *Floridante* Chrysander prints Rossane's aria "Dopo l'ombre" in B flat after a C major cadence. This aria was not in the original score.

wished to preserve his tonal freedom of action till the last possible moment, and so bring off a variety of surprises graded according to the nature of the context. To make almost every recitative end with a cadence on the dominant of the aria, regardless of what Handel wrote, as the editor of the new Halle full score of *Serse* does, is to practice the craft of Procrustes with a vengeance.

In Handel's mature operas the changes of scene are an integral part of the structure. Sometimes, not often, he wrote special music to cover them: for instance, the symphony for the assault on the city in Act I of *Radamisto* and the hunting chorus in Act II of *Deidamia*. These pieces are intended to accompany action, not to be heard as interludes; to lower the curtain, as modern directors are apt to do, is to break up the design. When there is a change of scene without linking music—a change in the modern sense, not the entry of a new character—Handel signalizes it through the tonality. As a rule we find a sharp break or shift, which assumes a dramatic and a structural function. In *Giulio Cesare* the second scene of Act I ends with Tolomeo denouncing the absent Caesar in the angry E flat major aria "L'empio, sleale." The action moves at once to Caesar's camp, where Caesar addresses the urn containing Pompey's ashes in G sharp minor. This progression—aria in E flat major, accompanied recitative in G sharp minor—recurs in Act II of *Lotario*, where, however, Handel is emphasizing a dramatic contrast without a change of scene. In Act III of *Giulio Cesare* Cleopatra, defeated, captured, and believing her lover dead, laments her fate in the E major aria "Piangerò la sorte mia" and goes out. Then comes a scene for Caesar, alive after all, beginning in the most unlikely key, F major. Bertarido's wonderful B flat minor arioso "Chi di voi," which opens the prison scene in *Rodelinda*, follows an aria for his enemy Grimoaldo in A minor. The whole effect of these surprises (and there are many more) depends on the continuity of the action; it is destroyed if the curtain falls or if there is a pause for the audience to chatter. The basis is the quick scene change. Handel was not the only composer to link this with tonality; Mozart did the same.

If Handel had had to cater for a falling curtain and the interruptions enforced by it, he would have planned his operas differently; so would the librettists. It may well be that the applause or catcalls of the audience sometimes spoiled his effects in performance. That has happened, and still happens, in later opera. But it does not follow that he had no such effects in mind. It would be characteristic of him to forge organic links that might escape notice, just as he articulated most of his oratorios as dramatic unities although he knew he would never see them acted.

His shaping of whole scenes deserves closer attention. Here perhaps is the most striking evidence of his skill as a theatrical craftsman and the trouble he took to make music and action mutually supporting, though the fact that it concerns long stretches of music makes the point difficult to demonstrate outside the theater. While studying it we can observe his growing mastery of the medium. He began by accommodating himself to the practises of his age; he went on to transcend them.

His first opera, *Almira*, illustrates the librettists' choice of an initial tableau or dramatic climax as a means of projecting the listener into the story with the impetus of a swimmer plunging off a diving-board. It begins with the coronation of the young queen in the amphitheater of Valladolid. There is a great procession of courtiers, bodyguards, soldiers, and people, with officials carrying the insignia and a military band of trumpets and drums filling the balconies. They play a Rejouissance or flourish on stage, and after the ceremony accompany a brief chorus of acclamation. This leads to a ballet of Spanish ladies and gentlemen, after which the characters in turn react to the situation, and the exit arias begin. The drama is successfully launched, but the credit belongs to the librettist rather than to Handel, whose music does not add much.

Nor does he greatly illumine the review of the Christian army before Jerusalem that begins *Rinaldo*, or the battle that is supposed to rage offstage throughout the first act of *Teseo*. Here, according to the libretto, "the Curtain rises at the Sound of a Warlike Symphony; and behind the Scenes there is heard the Noise of Men fighting." Handel does not supply a symphony, unless we count the last movement of the overture, which is not at all warlike; one would never know a battle was in progress if the characters did not refer to it from time to time. *Silla* opens with another lost opportunity: a Roman triumph, with the dictator, fresh from his victory over Marius, passing under a triumphal arch in a chariot drawn by Negro slaves, preceded by lictors with fasces and consular ensigns and followed by a train of fettered kings, all to the sound of military instruments. There is no music for this; an unfortunate omission, since the plot depends on Silla's arrogant and un-Roman ostentation on this occasion, which shocks the other characters. It is possible, however, that the published scores of both these operas are incomplete, since the autographs are defective or lost.

From the Royal Academy period on Handel misses no tricks of this kind. Whether or not the libretto opens on a climax, as it usually does, he rarely fails to increase its impact by some structural manipulation of the music. In a number of operas he and his theater poet forwarded the process by improving upon the source libretto. One of his most successful gambits is to make the overture overlap the first scene. The typical French overture of the period, to which Handel conforms in all his operas, has a slow stately movement in double-dotted rhythm, a more or less fugal Allegro, and one or sometimes two dance movements. In at least six operas, by making the curtain rise early, Handel treats the last movement of the overture as the first of the action, which is under way before the audience is prepared for it. The famous minuet in the overture to *Arianna*, which was played with the curtain up, accompanies the disembarcation of the Minotaur's chosen victims in the port of Knossos. There is a powerful irony in the use of this lovely tune, enriched by the unexpected entry of the horns, as background to such a tragic procession.

Three times Handel replaces the dance movement with a march, always with reference to what is happening on the stage. In *Scipione* it inaugurates a spectacular triumph scene, rather like that in *Silla*, with the Roman army followed by slaves and captives of both sexes entering through an arch. In a stately arioso in G major, the key of the overture, Scipio proclaims his victory over Spain and looks forward to subduing Egypt. He congratulates his army in recitative, bestows various honors, and is offered the most beautiful of the captives, Berenice, with whom he promptly falls in love. When she begs him to protect her virtue, he reassures her in what sounds like a new aria in E minor. But it turns out to be the second part of his G major arioso, which he repeats as a da capo. Handel has bound the whole scene together (including the overture) in a unity of action and tonality, set the plot in motion, sketched two of the three principal characters, and extended the confines of da capo form by including a long section of recitative between the first part and the second.

The march in the overture to *Ezio* introduces another triumph, the return of the hero from his victory over Attila, "preceded by martial Instruments, Slaves and Ensigns of the vanquished, and followed by his victorious Soldiers." He is received by the Emperor Valentiniano on his throne, the Praetorian Guard, and the people. The Emperor embraces Ezio and sings an aria of congratulation, but no sooner has he left the stage than the ceremony is turned to irony by the machinations of conspiracy. Metastasio has thirty lines of recitative between the overture and Ezio's return. Handel quickens the drama by introducing him before the end of the overture. In *Deidamia* the march is played by a band of brass and drums at the back of the stage on board the ship from which Ulysses and the other Greek ambassadors are landing on Scyros to look for Achilles, whose aid the oracle has declared essential to the capture of Troy.

Other openings are still more dramatic. The minuet in the overture to *Giulio Cesare* suddenly becomes a chorus as Caesar and his army, crossing "an old Bridge over a Branch of the Nile" at Alexandria, are welcomed by the Egyptians. The choral parts were sung by the other soloists, presumably from the wings, and the curtain must have been raised at the beginning of the minuet or (perhaps more effectively) in the middle. The chorus was an insertion of Handel's; it is not in the source libretto.

In *Admeto* the third movement of the overture, marked "Lentemento," is a ballet. The dancers represent the specters tormenting the troubled sleep of the dying Admetus. He starts up and implores them to stop in a remarkable accompanied recitative and arioso, with the orchestra alternating between adagio and agitato e furioso and the voice entering *con stupore*. Act II of this opera has a second and equally impressive overture, followed by an accompanied recitative and another symphony. This scene too was danced and mimed. It represents the rescue of Alcestis from Hades by Hercules. The stage directions describe it as follows: "Hell in which is seen Alceste chain'd to a Rock and tormented by two Furies. This Scene opens to the Sound of a Symphony, which Strikes Terror. Hercules, with his Club, who leads about Cerberus in a Chain. [Presently] he throws Cerberus into a deep Abyss, out of which issues a great Quantity of Smoke and Flames." During the second symphony he "descends into the Abyss, beats the Furies with his Club . . . who being all struck with Fear, fly on their Wings thro' the Air, and go out of the Summit of the Cave." The music, which suggests a compound of Bach at his most chromatic and the pulsating intensity of Gluck, is as startling as the dramatic conception, and fully capable of striking terror.

   Riccardo Primo and *Tolomeo* both begin, like Verdi's *Otello*, with a storm off the coast of Cyprus, followed by a shipwreck. In each overture Handel substitutes an accompanied recitative, running straight on, for the dance movement. In *Tolomeo* the hero, about to commit suicide in the belief that his wife is dead, sees a landingcraft capsize in the surf and stops to rescue its occupant, who turns out to be his brother. The *Riccardo* recitative is an astonishing movement, a pictorial symphony with the voices breaking in towards the end. Handel uses drums with strings and oboes (no brass) and contrasted dynamics in English—soft, very soft, loud—to suggest the thunderclaps and their distant echoes. The effect is highly impressionistic, and not unlike the storm scenes in some of Méhul's operas. As the thunder dies away, a beautiful transition leads to a great tragic aria in which Costanza, saved by an apparent miracle, despairs of the survival of her shipmates and her future husband.

   Several of the later operas start with an arresting tableau: *Partenope* with the founding of Naples, *Giustino* with the coronation of a Byzantine Emperor and his consort ("a Band of Instruments on the Stage," according to the libretto), *Berenice* with the Queen of Egypt and her satraps giving diplomatic audience to the Roman ambassador, *Sosarme* with a military review in the great square of Sardis followed by a sortie of the half-starved garrison, *Faramondo* with the consecration of an oath of perpetual vengeance before a heathen idol, *Siroe* with the disinheriting of the heir to the throne of Persia in the Temple of the Sun.

   Three operas plunge from the overture into the height of a battle. In *Poro*, where an accompanied recitative again replaces the dance movement, the defeated hero attempts suicide. The German leader in *Arminio* is persuaded by his wife to save her from capture by flight, and the first number in the opera is a duet of despair. The opening scene of *Alessandro* seems to invite the talents of Hollywood. As the curtain rises Alexander the Great, at the head of a besieging army, "by the means of a Scaling Engine, mounts the Walls" of the city of Oxidraca, proclaiming himself the son of Jupiter. "The Besieg'd fly at the Approach of Alexander. . . . He throws himself within the Wall: The Besieged rally thither again, and repulse the Besiegers back with their Scaling-Machine." Leonatus and another force of Macedonians enter "with a Batt'ring Ram to demolish the Wall. . . . the Wall tumbles; and Alexander is seen among a Heap of slaughter'd Enemies, and defending himself against others, who are put to Flight by Leonatus, and his Macedonians." Handel deals with this in two military symphonies on the same material, with trumpets added to the second and some declamatory recitative for Alexander in the middle. The music is nothing out of the way, but it is effective as a background to the action, and it establishes Alexander as a leader brave to the point of recklessness. The battles were enacted with a fair degree of realism; the noise is said to have carried from the Haymarket to Charing Cross, a distance of several hundred yards. Some continental opera houses, including Vienna and Dresden, had special functionaries whose job was to direct the stage fighting, but there is no evidence that they existed in London.

The music of these opening scenes has more variety of form and texture than we find in the body of the operas. Handel generally picks out the main dramatic issue in an accompanied recitative, and on several occasions incorporates a short chorus or symphonic movement, so that he is well into the plot before the exit arias begin. In all but the latest operas these choruses were sung not by an extra body of singers but by the soloists as a group, on or off stage, reinforced as a rule by trumpets or horns. We know this from the autographs, where Handel wrote the names of the singers against the parts, as in the coro at the end of the opera. Sometimes this produces amusing results, as when after the capture of Oxidraca Alexander, not uncharacteristically perhaps, leads the praises of his own glory. Elsewhere it involves apparent contradictions in the plot. The Egyptian welcome to Caesar in *Giulio Cesare*, and still more the chorus proclaiming Berengario King of Italy in *Lotario* and the *coro militare* that occurs twice in *Sosarme*, have a nonsensical aspect, since some of the singers named have to shout against their own side. Whether they sang from the wings (like the dead basses in the finales of *Flavio* and *Sosarme*) or hoisted false colors for the occasion we cannot be sure. The former seems more probable. What is certain is that Handel set such a high value on these choruses as a dramatic feature—their music is always very simple—that he forced his soloists into service as a group. Their notorious vanity may not have been flattered.

Choruses of this type are not confined to opening scenes. Handel employs them elsewhere as early as *Agrippina* and *Teseo*, where a chorus precipitates a crisis by hailing Theseus as King while hs father is still alive. Similar movements celebrate Partenope's victory over the King of Cumae, Atalanta's prowess in a boar hunt, and Richard Coeur-de-Lion's assault on the walls of Limissus; here the voices utter a warcry at the beginning of a battle symphony. In later acts of *Giulio Cesare* and *Alessandro* the soloists not on stage have to represent a chorus of conspirators, though Chrysander has suppressed the evidence in the score of *Alessandro* and misled Dent into crediting Alexander's army with a squadron of soprano soldiers. In *Giulio Cesare* the conspirators enter very dramatically during the final ritornello of one of Caesar's arias as he goes off to face them. These brief concerted pieces never amount to much as music, but their effect in an opera seria context is out of all proportion to the means employed.

When the libretto does not begin with a tableau or an action piece, Handel still contrives something unusual in the musical design if he possibly can. The long and beautifully managed first scene of *Radamisto* is set before a besieged city, but though the walls, the encircling river with its fortified bridge, and the camp of the besiegers are all in view, the stage is empty except for Polissena, the rejected wife of Tiridate, "sitting at a Table before the Door of her Tent." Again Handel suppresses the overture's dance movement, substituting a bleak arioso in which Polissena, with an unaccompanied cry based on the interval of a tritone, implores the protection of the gods. This scene builds up more in the manner of later opera. The other characters are introduced quite naturally, the different strands of the plot are exposed in a series of strong situations, and the scene ends with a military symphony as the besiegers assault the bridge.

In *Tamerlano,* as befits the somber subject, the curtain rises on a prison where the Emperor Bajazet stands loaded with chains. Handel composed several versions of this scene, all of exceptional quality. It is revealing of his self-criticism, the fertility of his genius, and his sense of dramatic proportion that he rejected pages of magnificent music and settled on the simplest version of all. Something similar happened in the first scene of *Floridante.* Elmira has gone hunting to be near her lover Floridante, who is away on a campaign, and in an arioso expresses her hope of seeing him. When she learns in recitative that he has been victorious she repeats her arioso, without its ritornello and with the words modified: her hope is closer to fulfillment. That is how the music stands in the score: another variant of the da capo principle. But Handel first composed the scene as a rondo, ABACA, a full da capo aria followed by recitative and then a second da capo with the changed words. He probably shortened this because it held up the action. *Imeneo* also begins with an arioso repeated after recitative, the second time enriched by additional string parts in the coda. It is a most beautiful piece, the lament of a lover for his lost beloved, and it prepares the way for the moving end of the opera not only in mood but in tonality. The overture and the whole opening scene, and several important pieces later, establish G major as a tonic; the final coro, with its undertones of tragedy (Tirinto has found Rosmene but lost her again), settles instead in the relative minor.

Rodelinda and *Lotario* present an exposition which is in all essentials the cavatina-cabaletta layout of romantic opera: a slow arioso, a recitative episode that materially alters the dramatic balance, and a brilliant quick aria in a related key in which the same character reacts to the new situation and goes out. Rodelinda's "cavatina"—it was originally a full aria, but Handel cut it down to an arioso before the first performance—is a lament for the loss of her husband, combined with a resolve to live for the sake of their child. The usurper Grimoaldo offers to restore her to the throne if she will marry him; she indignantly refuses (cabaletta). By the end of this short scene Handel has established the character of his heroine and the central motives of the plot. In *Lotario* it is the tyrant Berengario whose acquaintance we make at the outset: his gnawing ambition in the magnificent arioso, and his fury in the aria after his will has been thwarted. These cavatina-cabaletta designs are not uncommon in Handel's operas, early as well as late, nor are they confined to the beginning of a scene. They hinge on the fact that an arioso did not entail an obligatory exit. Unless he can be shown to have been anticipated, it is possible that Handel was adding something vital not only to opera seria but to the main stream of operatic development. Many of the ariosos, nearly all quiet pieces in slow tempo and of incomparable beauty, were his own interpolations into the librettos.[9] Nor is there any doubt about the musical and tonal unity that the whole complex (arioso–recitative–aria) acquired at his hands.

Three operas have nocturnal openings in which the music echoes the romantic overtones of the drama. Amadigi, lost in the magic garden of the sorceress Melissa, appeals to night to aid his escape, but his efforts are disrupted by sorcery.[10] The aria begins with a wonderful G minor Largo in 3/4, breaks into an F major ritornello (Allegro 3/8) when Amadigi's escape is blocked by two troops of infernal spirits, and is never finished. It drops first into accompanied recitative, then into secco, destroying the expected da capo sequence and pushing the action forward. The dramatic frustration is reflected in the design and underlined by the tonality.

The first scene of *Flavio* comprises a recitative and duet for two lovers in a garden; Vitige slips out of Teodata's bedroom under cover of darkness, and they utter a lingering farewell—an episode that suggests *Romeo and Juliet* or even *Tristan* rather than the traditional image of opera seria. More memorable as music is the great accompanied recitative that begins *Orlando* (example 27, pp. 138–139). In a mountain landscape at night the magician Zoroastro is discovered "leaning on a Stone, and contemplating the Motion of the Stars" in order to foretell the destiny of the hero torn between the passions of love and war. Handel was to find further employment for the staccato violin figure in Lichas's aria "No longer, fate, relentless frown" in *Hercules*.

These opening scenes have been discussed at length because they represent a structurally successful element in opera seria and bring out

[9] See p. 42 above.
[10] His aria is preceded by a short scene with Dardano that somewhat weakens its impact.

the quality of Handel's response to the challenge. Each is calculated to strike the appropriate mood, whether heroic, romantic, or (in the case of "Ombra mai fù" in *Serse*) half ironical, for the opera to come. To a lesser extent Handel follows a similar line in the intermediate acts. These often begin with an arioso or, especially in the later operas, with an orchestral movement, sometimes (as in Act II of *Ezio*) linked with an accompanied recitative but seldom involving much in the way of stage action. The moonrise symphony in *Ariodante* is an outstanding example of a few bars setting the scene for what follows in a manner we associate with the romantic age. It disproves Eisenschmidt's statement that there is nothing pictorial or programmatic about the symphonic movements in Handel's operas.

At the end of a scene, and particularly at the end of an act (excluding for the moment the last act), Handel has to employ a different technique. He is faced with a dramatic diminuendo, but must aim at an impression of finality rather than anticlimax. These concluding movements are usually full da capo arias. Handel took a lot of trouble over them, often placing the finest music in the opera at the end of an act, and it is astonishing how much variety he achieves. Sometimes he writes a long, brilliant, and richly scored aria for a star singer, who is then triumphantly carried off by the applause of the audience. The arias that end Act I of *Silla* (with trumpet obbligato), Act II of *Scipione*, and Act I of *Alcina* could scarcely fail in this. When the drama is static, Handel exerts himself to create a musical climax, as in the superb simile aria that ends Act II of *Lotario*. This is slow in tempo, but marvelously rich in texture, harmony, and lyrical suspense, with every ritornello varied. Another beautiful example ends Act I of *Radamisto*.

He naturally prefers a musical and a dramatic climax to coincide. Once or twice the librettist makes this easy, as in the great second-act finales of *Alcina* and *Orlando*. Both are scenes of violent emotional upheaval, and in each case Handel builds a substantial structure, combining an accompanied recitative of exceptional range and elaboration with a crowning aria. The recitative discharges the emotion; the aria reconcentrates it in different terms. Elsewhere he incorporates a sharp conflict of mood within the aria, as in Selene's "Si poco è forte" at the end of Act II of *Berenice*, where he sets a long serene melody in 9/8 against

Example 27

a fierce Allegro second part in 4/4. Or he sums up one of the central
issues of the plot: Lucejo in Act I of *Scipione* tormented by the fear
of jealousy, or Andronico in Act I of *Tamerlano* compelled to conceal
his love for Asteria but feeling it all the more—a magnificent aria
introduced by an equally fine accompanied recitative in cyclic form.[11]

Alternatively he may give a new twist to the drama by manipulat-
ing the mood, texture, design, or tonality in such a way that the concluding aria brings a shock of surprise. Act II of *Flavio* is mainly light
in tone, but it turns to tragedy at the end when Emilia finds her father
killed by her lover. She wants to avenge him, but cannot face the
prospect and decides to die herself. The effect of her F sharp minor
Largo "Mà chi punir desio?" with its semitone clashes and double
suspensions after so much gay and charming music is overwhelming.
Several times Handel places a passionate aria in a minor key after a
string of cheerful pieces in the major. Lucejo's jealous outburst in
Scipione follows three arias in the major; so does Bertarido's B minor
aria in Act I of *Rodelinda*, where he believes his wife is unfaithful and
decides to trap her. In Act I of *Amadigi* the hero closes with a G minor
Largo, begging fate to restore his beloved or let him die, after four
arias in the major; and Handel strengthens the contrast by using a bare
texture of unison violins and bass after giving the other four arias a
particularly rich accompaniment. Act I of *Giustino* has an even more
striking climax, an intensely chromatic D minor Largo for Arianna,
who is about to be thrown to a sea monster and prays for a speedy
death, after no fewer than seven consecutive pieces in major keys, all
but the first in quick tempi. It is impossible to appreciate this sort of
long-term planning outside the context of the whole act, and easy for
the reader of the score to miss it altogether.

Handel sometimes crowns an intermediate act with a duet, and
once (Act I of *Orlando*) with a trio. On these occasions he holds the
action suspended, the situation unresolved; the characters go off in
opposite directions. These movements are all of outstanding quality,
especially the duets in a minor key and slow tempo where a pair of

[11] Both are new in Handel's libretto. In Piovene's, set by Gasparini in 1710, the
act ends tamely with a scene for Asteria and her confidante.

lovers or a married couple bid each other an agonized farewell under the threat of death or torture. Such are the F sharp minor largo duets that end the second acts of *Rodelinda* and *Tolomeo* (which are so alike that Handel exchanged them in revivals of the operas) and the duet at the end of Act I of *Floridante*. There is another in Act III of *Tamerlano*, but it closes a scene, not an act. The lament of the widowed Cornelia and her son Sesto in Act I of *Giulio Cesare* belongs to the same class, as does the *Orlando* trio, in which two characters try in vain to console the broken heart of the third. That, however, is in a major key. All these movements make a satisfying conclusion in the theater, and they are the nearest approach in Handel to the concerted finales of later opera.

Once or twice the plan is varied. The duet that ends Act II of *Faramondo*, which exceptionally, and significantly, is an extended arioso without da capo, projects the interest forward into the next act. Rosimonda, having released Faramondo from captivity and given him back his sword, sends him away for his own safety. He is reluctant to go, since he loves her; without giving any positive encouragement, she offers him the luxury of hope. Act II of *Ottone* culminates in one of Handel's rare duets for two women characters (there are only three duets for women and three for men in all his operas).[12] Adelberto's mother and bride, having smuggled him out of prison through a secret passage, thank the dark night for favoring their stratagem—another romantic conception. The most remarkable of these duet-finales concludes Act I of *Poro*. Alexander the Great has defeated the Indian King Poro, and fallen in love with Cleofide, who is betrothed to Poro. Early in the act Cleofide and Poro each sing an aria pledging eternal constancy. But Cleofide rather tactlessly tries to wheedle Alexander with fair words and tears. In the duet Poro accuses her of infidelity and she reproaches him with groundless jealousy. Each begins with a bitterly ironical quotation from the other's aria, words and music, and Handel combines both with fresh material in a masterstroke of musical drama, for which Metastasio must share the credit.

---

[12] The other duets for women are in *Alessandro* and *Arminio;* those for men in *Tamerlano, Berenice,* and *Imeneo.*

In the late operas *Imeneo* and *Deidamia* Handel finishes an intermediate act with a chorus in the modern sense, not an ensemble of
soloists. This may reflect oratorio practice, but it appears to have little
dramatic significance; in two instances out of three he brings back
earlier material simply (it would seem) to round things off. *Ariodante*
is more interesting. In this opera he evolved a new type of finale—or
rather two distinct types; and they are worth describing, since the
defects of Chrysander's edition have led modern writers astray.

In all four of his opera productions in the Covent Garden season
of 1734/1735 (revivals of *Il Pastor Fido* and *Arianna*, and the newly
composed *Ariodante* and *Alcina*) Handel made considerable use of
chorus and ballet. This was the accidental result of his move to Covent
Garden, where a ballet had already been engaged, but he took characteristic advantage of the opportunity. He composed the first two acts
of *Ariodante* between August 12 and September 9, 1734, without any
dance music and with two of the parts written for voices of different
pitch from those that subsequently sang them. At this stage Act I
ended with a duet for Ginevra and Ariodante followed by a chorus
on the same theme, and Act II with Ginevra's aria "Il mio crudel
martoro." Some time between September 9 and October 24, when he
finished the opera, Handel learned of the availability of the ballet and
introduced it into all three finales, going back to alter the first two.
To that of Act I he appended four dances, one of them based on the
melody of the duet and chorus, and marked a repeat of the chorus at
the end, producing an extended sequence of movements in related keys
with a thematic link running right through. Before the production of
Ariodante he did exactly the same thing with the third-act finales of *Il
Pastor Fido* and *Arianna*, the two revivals, inserting a suite of dances
between the last aria and the coro, which already employed the same
theme, and basing one of the dances on this as well. Chrysander confused the two 1734 revivals of *Il Pastor Fido,* the first of which included
the choruses but not the dances, and omitted all the dances in *Arianna*
except one, which he printed in the wrong place. The first finale of
Ariodante, with its ballet and chorus, may be one of the rare exceptions to the rule that the curtain did not drop between the acts, though

the license seems to have been used to reveal a spectacular or crowded scene rather than to close one.

Handel's revised second-act finale for *Ariodante* was still more original. In her tragic E minor aria Ginevra, falsely accused of unchastity, begins to doubt her sanity and invokes death to end her sufferings. In the added ballet she falls into an exhausted sleep, and two groups of dancers representing good and bad dreams enter in turn and engage in a combat that enacts visually the struggle in her mind. She wakes in terror, and the act ends abruptly with a six-bar accompanied recitative in F sharp minor—the only thing of the kind in any of Handel's operas, though he had experimented with recitative endings, in and out of the main key, in several early cantatas.

This scene does not appear in Chrysander's edition of *Ariodante*. Instead he prints an entry of Moors, which fits neither the dramatic situation nor the locality (Edinburgh), and a rondeau. The dream ballet and the accompanied recitative he gives as an alternative end to Act II of *Alcina*,[13] though the cue at the beginning is the close of Ginevra's aria, which he apparently failed to recognize. In the event there was no ballet in Act II of *Ariodante* at its first production in January 1735, perhaps because the opera was already very long. But Ginevra's dream deserves to be restored to its context.[14] Chrysander's remark that it is more appropriate to Alcina, a heroine of a very different type, shows that he misunderstood both operas. The end with ballet and accompanied recitative seems to have been Handel's idea. It does not occur in the 1718 Venice edition of Salvi's libretto, on which Handel's was based, though the possibility that there was some intermediate version cannot be ruled out.

In two operas, on each occasion in the second act, Handel employed the characteristic diminuendo effect of the opera seria scene-plan as part of a larger whole, to build up a theatrical situation of gripping power. The action rises to a dramatic confrontation, with all

[13] It is possible that Handel at some time thought of using it here. If so, he rejected the idea.

[14] As it was in the first English stage performance since Handel's, at the Barber Institute of Fine Arts, Birmingham, in 1964.

the characters on stage; this is followed by a succession of exit arias until one of them is left alone. Instead of the tension evaporating it is prolonged and developed; and the fact that this appears to run against the grain of the opera produces a design of exceptional tautness unattainable outside the opera seria convention. In both contexts the tension is sustained for the greater part of an act.

The first occurs in the Venetian opera *Agrippina*. The Emperor Claudio has conquered Britain with the aid of Ottone, who has also saved his life. In return Claudio has promised him the succession. But Agrippina, Claudio's wife, covets the throne for Nero, her son by a former husband. She knows that Ottone and Claudio are competitors for the favors of Poppea, who returns Ottone's love, and uses this knowledge to further her schemes. She tells Poppea that Ottone has agreed to give her up to Claudio, in return for the succession, and suggests that if she wants revenge she should pretend to accede to Claudio's desires on condition that he disinherits Ottone. Poppea falls into the trap. This is the situation at the start of Act II, which leads up to Claudio's triumphal entry to celebrate his victory. There is a great deal of irony in the early part of the scene, since everyone except Ottone has something to conceal and Agrippina dare not let Poppea discover the truth, that Ottone is innocent. The climax is a substantial "chorus," with trumpets and drums, in which the Emperor is acclaimed by the other seven soloists. Then the exits begin. When Ottone asks for his promised reward, Claudio denounces him as a traitor. Thunderstruck, Ottone appeals in turn to Agrippina, Poppea, and Nero. Each rejects him, answering his single line of recitative in a short aria without initial ritornello and in a different key, and goes out. The three minor characters follow their example in recitative, and Ottone, deserted by everyone without knowing why, pours out his bitterness and grief in an accompanied recitative and aria of superb eloquence, the greatest music in the opera.

In *Tamerlano* the plan is similar, but the emotional position is reversed: the character who remains on the stage moves from anguish to joy. The effect is even more impressive, since there are no minor characters to be disposed of in recitative, and all the music, not just the final aria, shows Handel at the height of his powers. Tamerlano, the Tartar conqueror, has overthrown and captured the Turkish Emperor Bajazet and his daughter Asteria. The Greek prince Andronico, Tamerlano's ally, falls in love with Asteria, and she with him. But Tamerlano, though he has promised to marry the Princess Irene, also loves Asteria and orders Andronico to intercede with her and her father on his behalf. Andronico dare not refuse, though he is confident that she will reject the proposal. Bajazet dismisses it with scorching contempt; but Asteria horrifies her father, her lover, and Irene by seeming to comply with the conqueror's wishes.

That is where the story stands before the second scene of Act II, which takes place in Tamerlano's throne room. He invites Asteria to mount the throne. The others, after a series of vain appeals and denunciations, all turn their backs on her. Even when Bajazet disowns her she makes no move; but when he threatens to kill himself she can bear it no longer. Rising from the throne, she throws at Tamerlano's feet the dagger with which she had planned to receive his first embrace. The tension, which has accumulated over a series of highly dramatic recitatives, secco and accompanied, is released in a trio in which Tamerlano furiously orders father and daughter to execution, a sentence they accept with equanimity, and storms out. Asteria asks Bajazet, Andronico, and Irene in turn, in one line of recitative, if they still think her an unworthy daughter, a faithless lover, a scheming rival. Each replies with a short aria in binary form and a different key and goes out. The first word, "No!" marked as recitative in the libretto, Handel each time incorporates in the aria. Asteria is left alone, and the act ends with a full-scale da capo aria in which she pours out her relief that she has not lost their love and respect.[15]

The scheme of the latter part of the scene is worth setting out in detail.

---

[15] This was a late substitution. Piovene's 1710 and 1719 librettos ended the act with a tragic aria, "Cor di padre e cor di amante." Handel set this in his first draft, but transferred it to the beginning of Act III, where it replaced an aria for Bajazet, "Sù la sponda del pigro Lete," of which two magnificent settings, both in B flat minor, are printed in Chrysander's appendix.

Trio (Tamerlano, Bajazet, Asteria)	D major (exit Tamerlano)	33 bars allegro* 4/4
Recitative (Asteria)	B major	3 bars
Aria (Bajazet)	E minor (exit)	62 bars 3/8
Recitative (Asteria)	E major–G♯ major	2 bars
Aria (Andronico)	E major (exit)	29 bars 4/4
Recitative (Asteria)	C minor–G major	2 bars
Aria (Irene)	G major (exit)	72 bars 3/8 (including 2 repeats)
Recitative (Asteria)	E♭ major–D major	8 bars
Aria (Asteria)	B♭ major (end of act)	254 bars (including da capo)

* This is the only tempo mark in the scene. Handel must have regarded the tempi of the next four movements as self-evident; and indeed it is not easy to imagine more than one satisfactory solution.

The trio and the first three arias follow the same outline: no ritornellos except at the end for the exit, and no da capo. The action moves swiftly forward, helped by Handel's subtle control of the tonality, which keeps the ear in suspense as to what key is coming next.[16] Only at the end is the music permitted to expand: the leisurely gait of Asteria's aria with its long ritornellos (twenty bars before the voice enters) and its unexpected key releases the pent-up emotion in her heart. On paper the scheme may appear simple, if not naive; it would be difficult to exaggerate its potency in the theater.

The overall plan is the same as in *Agrippina:* recitative building up to an ensemble—the outward climax—followed by a series of exit arias that clear the stage and focus attention on the character to whom they are addressed and whose mounting excitement finds vent in the final aria. This becomes the counterclimax toward which the whole scene has been moving. Some credit for this is due to the librettist, and the layout may have been employed in other operas before *Agrippina.* But the genius with which it is exploited, and its impact in its full context, which includes all we have learned of the characters from their previous

[16] Handel did not evolve this all at once. Chrysander (pp. 150, 84) prints earlier versions of the arias of Bajazet and Irene in different keys.

music, belong unquestionably to Handel. If he can bend the convention to such purpose, we have no right to dismiss his operas as obsolete.

One problem remains: the final scene of the last act. Here we come up against a major drawback of the opera seria convention, the statutory happy end with its coro for the soloists, nearly always a quatrain or two of perfunctory and platitudinous rejoicing. It would be wrong to condemn the happy end, which lasted long after Handel's day into the nineteenth century, as an inevitable anticlimax. It can be tolerable, and even satisfying, as we have seen in the antiheroic operas. This is also true of stories in which villainy is destroyed by overreaching itself, such as *Giulio Cesare, Sosarme,* and *Ariodante,* and of the best of the magic operas, *Orlando* and *Alcina.* The trouble comes when a plot with tragic implications is betrayed by a conclusion that rings false to the characters as hitherto presented; and the more vividly they have been realized in the music, the greater the shock we experience. The lustful and vicious tyrant suddenly sees the error of his ways, surrenders the woman he has been pursuing to her rightful owner, and takes back his long-suffering wife as if nothing had happened; whereupon everyone forgives him and shakes hands on it. This or a similar situation occurs in *Rodrigo, Silla, Radamisto, Tamerlano, Lotario,* and other heroic operas, some of them works of outstanding merit. Generally the change of heart comes at the last moment in a few lines of recitative; and the summary way in which the plot is tidied up seems bound to provoke a musical as well as a dramatic collapse.

It is clear that the librettists abandoned hope of making these finales dramatically convincing. In *Tolomeo* we never hear what happens to the two villains; each is narrowly prevented from carrying out a treacherous murder, yet after their exposure neither utters a word except to join cheerfully in the coro. In *Rinaldo* the conversion of Armida and Argante to Christianity is ludicrous, as Handel came to see in 1731 when he rewrote the end and kept them out of the coro. Some early operas (*Amadigi, Teseo, Il Pastor Fido*) make more or less clumsy use of a supernatural deus ex machina such as we find in Lully, Rameau, and Gluck. The libretto of *Rodelinda* is exceptional in taking pains to evade the difficulty by advance preparation. Grimoaldo, though a man of vicious impulses, is shown as a weakling without the courage of his convictions. He acts under the promptings of his counsellor Garibaldo, and his ultimate remorse and abdication, coinciding with Garibaldo's death, are less incredible than they would be otherwise.

Handel's treatment of the coro shows that over the years he became increasingly aware of its limitations and took steps to overcome them. He evolved two methods, one purely musical, the other musical and dramatic. The early operas end conventionally with a simple coro in dance rhythm and da capo form. Later he began to develop this into a substantial structure, over which he took obvious pains, sometimes modifying the source libretto or giving it a new end, as in all three of his Metastasio operas. The finale of *Radamisto* is an elaborate rondo with a full windband of oboes, bassoons, horns, and trumpets, including three duet episodes for pairs of soloists in contrasted keys and, in the first version, a ballet as well. The dances, based on the music of the coro, have recently come to light and are still unpublished. The central section of the *Giulio Cesare* coro, very appropriately, is a duet for Caesar and Cleopatra with woodwind accompaniment. The last scene of *Alessandro* is unique. This is the first of the five operas in which Handel had the ticklish job of writing for the rival prima donnas Cuzzoni and Faustina. At the end each of the ladies in turn had a duet with Senesino, who played Alexander the Great. He can scarcely marry them both, so he offers one his love, the other his friendship. They accept and express their further satisfaction in a trio, after which the coro follows. These four movements—two duets, trio, and coro—are thematically linked in one big finale, varied and strengthened by the scoring. The first duet is accompanied by first violins and bass only; the second, on a new theme in the dominant but running straight on, by two treble recorders, two violins, and bass. The trio, beginning in the dominant and moving back to the tonic, takes up the material of the first duet, which is further developed in the coro and reinforced by the full orchestra, including oboes, horns, and trumpets. This spacious design was Handel's own; the libretto prints both duets as recitative.

After 1731 Handel gave more and more weight to his finales. Eight consecutive operas, and three more later, show him going out of his way to build a satisfying climax, generally by linking the coro with the previous movement. In *Poro* he ends with a love duet and coro on the same material, the voices in the duet being picked out each with its own instrumental color and then treated in canon. *Ezio* has a quintuple finale on a single theme, which is sung as an arioso in binary form by the four principal characters in turn, differently scored and sometimes varied; for example the bass begins by singing the bass of the melody, but soon diverges and supplies a new and independent counterpoint. In the fifth section, the coro proper, the tune is divided between the voices but complete in the orchestra, now strengthened by the horns. The whole scheme is tonally unified, the first, third, and fifth sections being in the tonic, the second in the dominant, and the fourth in the relative minor. Each has its own set of words. The result is something between a rondo and a vaudeville like that in Mozart's *Entführung*. Metastasio ended with a straightforward coro in praise of innocence.

Sosarme and *Orlando* have exceptionally long and developed finales. That of *Sosarme*, in 9/8 time, retains the da capo but is treated with great flexibility and freedom of modulation; the second part moves from D minor to E major and ends in A minor, on which the opening returns in F major. *Orlando* has another vaudeville rondo with the voices, in ones and twos and all together, singing episodes based on the main theme in different keys, and a new melody in contrasted rhythm introduced halfway through. The libretto prints the text as two movements, a quartet followed by a coro. In *Ariodante* and *Alcina* the coro is based on the theme of the final dance in a ballet, which leads into it without a break. In *Arianna*, *Faramondo*, and *Serse* the last aria—a sublimely beautiful one in *Arianna* and *Serse*—lends its melody for expanded treatment in the coro. *Giustino* ends with another multiple movement, in which all acclaim the return of the golden age invoked by the chorus in the opening scene of the opera. The libretto calls it a quintet and chorus; Handel once more treats it as a unity, beginning with the soloists singly and in pairs. *Atalanta*, with its string of choruses and symphonies, its fanfares and fireworks in honor of the Prince of Wales, has the most spectacular finale of all, inspired of course by the festive occasion.

This elaboration satisfies the musical need for a climax, and may help to hide dramatic weaknesses, but it cannot compensate for a happy end that defies belief. In some operas, whose librettos seem to have outraged his sense of the dignity of human nature, Handel found a most original solution. He wrote the music demanded by the situation as he saw it, not by the words, whose sense he ignored. He seems to step outside the story in order to leave the sympathy of the audience where he feels it ought to rest; a higher artistic criterion assuredly bears him out. Six of his operas end in minor keys, and every one reflects a situation of this type. In *Amadigi*, *Tamerlano*, and *Arminio* the character who has most engaged Handel's sympathy—and therefore ours—is dead, in the first two cases by suicide. Melissa and Bajazet have magnificent death scenes on stage, and the bleak end in the minor, contradicting the text, places the weighty support of the composer behind our conviction that the vacuously cheerful coro is an artistic solecism. In *Poro*, *Berenice*, and *Imeneo* the librettist makes the more attractive of the two lovers surrender the heroine to his rival.[17] This may not have been the effect intended, but it is certainly how Handel takes it. By as it were muting the final rejoicings, he leaves us with the memory of the human suffering that underlies them.

The finales of *Tamerlano* and *Imeneo* in particular are profoundly moving in the theater. That of *Tamerlano* has a flavor almost of Shakespearian tragedy. The words are transcended by the music, which sets an ironical question mark against the very idea of a happy end. There is another point, which Chrysander conceals by marking the top vocal line for soprano. It is an alto part, sung by Irene. Neither the soprano nor the tenor sings in the coro. The tenor, Bajazet, is dead, and the soprano, Asteria, has collapsed with grief. The only voices are three altos and a bass, and Handel uses this dark coloring to reinforce his message. The text says in summary: "From this night of black torment and sorrow a fair day will dawn." There is nothing to suggest a fair day dawning in the music, which though in da capo form does not even introduce a contrast in the second part.

Handel was something of a specialist in these superimposed emo-

[17] *Poro* illustrates the point less convincingly than the other five operas, since Alexander is not wholly sympathetic; but he is a generous victor, whereas Poro is both jealous and treacherous.

tional patterns and ambiguous ends, whether or not they are implicit in the libretto. No other composer seems to have achieved precisely this effect. It recurs in the oratorios, three of which turn platitude into tragedy or doubt by ending in the minor. The supreme example is *Theodora,* where the complacent reflections of Morell on the martyrdom of Theodora and Didymus are transformed into one of the most moving finales in dramatic music. The threatened anticlimax turns out to be a climax, whose impact is if anything heightened by the discovery that words and music are pulling in opposite directions. It is never safe to condemn a Handel libretto without studying the score.

CHAPTER 9

Aria and Recitative

The principal unit in opera seria, the aria, demands consideration both as a musical form and as a means of dramatic expression, though the two aspects are in the last resort inseparable. The total number of arias in Handel's operas and Italian cantatas, including many still unpublished, must amount to something like two thousand, more than three times the number of Schubert's songs. They deserve a substantial monograph; only a few salient points can be touched on here.[1]

The first is the incredible fertility of Handel's melodic invention. Probably few people familiar with his operas would deny him the title of the greatest melodist in musical history, both for the number of beautiful tunes and for their variety, in mood, shape, span, harmonic implication, and rhythm. He is one of the few composers who could write a satisfactory full-length aria consisting of melody and nothing else, the instruments doubling the voice in unison or at the octave. "Bel piacere" in *Agrippina* owes its fascination partly to the compound rhythm, which vacillates unpredictably between 3/8 and 2/4 time (and in the second part, by means of hemiola, 3/4 as well), and partly to the constant extension and renewal of the melody from its inner resources. The ritornellos at beginning and end are harmonized, but the voice, with the violins in unison, is unsupported (example 28).

Another early unison aria, "Hò un non sò che nel cor," has an added refinement. The melody, with its cunningly placed ninths in the first half, is irresistible. This time the ritornellos (there is none at the

[1] See Anthony Lewis, "Handel and the Aria," in *Proceedings of the Royal Musical Association 1958–1959*, pp. 95–107.

Example 28

+ Violini tutti unis.

Bel pia — ce-re è go — de-re fi- do a — mor! que-sto fà — con-

ten-to il cor, questo fà — con-tento il cor, fà con — ten-to il cor.

beginning) are all short four-bar phrases in bare octaves—until the very end, after the da capo, when Handel obtains a startlingly rich and delightful effect by expanding the four bars to eight and the unison to two-part harmony, and crowning the whole with the leaping ninth from the first half, hitherto the property of the voice.[2]

This artistry was not attained without effort. Handel was a German, with perhaps an innate feeling for counterpoint and the harmonic implications of melody, but not for long melodic spans, as his earliest music shows. In Italy he assimilated the flexibility and eloquence of Scarlatti's vocal idiom, and the polished energy of the instrumental style of Corelli; later he added something from English composers, notably Purcell. We can watch him forging his tools in the hundred-odd cantatas composed during the Italian years; they are full of bold experiments and contain the seeds of everything that came later. He emerged as a master of the melodic paragraph, built up from the initial cell (which may be quite short) by a process of self-generation, involving internal rhythmic variation, unsymmetrical phrase-lengths, misplaced accents, interrupted cadences, contrapuntal friction, and much else. Above all, and this of course is its justification, it sounds perfectly spontaneous. When he writes what looks like a four-bar phrase, it may turn out to be a combination of two uneven units, $1\frac{1}{2} + 2\frac{1}{2}$, as in the beautiful melody "Bella sorge la speranza" in *Arianna*. The rhythmic subtleties implicit in the ritornello multiply when the voice enters; the second strain (bars 6–10), after one echoing bar, is expanded into a paragraph of thirteen bars, divided by the voice in the proportion $2 + 11$ (example 29, pp. 154–155).

[2] This aria was composed for *La Resurrezione*. When Handel used it again in *Agrippina* and *Il Pastor Fido* he omitted this coda.

Example 29

Another constant element, except in the unison pieces, is counterpoint. When the aria has nothing but a voice part and a bass, the two lines are sure to interact on each other with fruitful results. Handel's basses are scarcely ever a mere prop; they are active and functional. In *Almira* and other early works they are sometimes too active, so that they dwarf the vocal line or detract from it. Many arias have an instrumental texture of four, five, or more real parts, with the voice standing out like a soloist in a concerto. In his own day Handel was accused of drowning the singers with complicated and noisy accompaniments. This charge suggests that those who made it were nightingale fanciers, and that other composers' accompaniments must have been distressingly thin; for Handel seldom fails to ensure that the voice will cut through, either by marking down the dynamics and simplifying the orchestral figuration or, more typically, by confining the upper instruments to the interstices of the vocal line. There is an aria in *Giustino* ("Allor ch'io forte avrò") where the violins enjoy the melodic cream while the voice—a castrato too—enters with an inner part. (This is one of the pieces reflecting the "modern" Neapolitan style.) But such instances are very rare. Handel does not follow Bach's practice of treating the obbligato instrument on a parity with the voice in a closely woven texture. A logical pattern was never his chief consideration.

The standard form of the da capo aria in Handel, insofar as there is such a thing, comprises a first part with ritornello at beginning and end and subsidiary ritornellos between the vocal paragraphs, and a shorter second part founded on a related key, usually the relative minor or major, developing the material of the first and modulating more freely. As a rule the second part has no ritornello of its own, though it may find a new way back to the da capo and so modify the opening. It is generally in the same meter and tempo as the first part, and similarly or more lightly scored. Sometimes Handel exploits a different part of the singer's compass, more often in a lower but occasionally in a higher range. The first part of the bigger arias falls into sections in related keys, based on the principal theme and associated with the subsidiary ritornellos; the keys differ from those of the second part, so that a satisfactory tonal balance is preserved over the whole aria.

No sooner has this been stated than aria after aria leaps up as an exception. Every one of the features mentioned, and others besides, is subject to variation. The possibilities are practically limitless, though all depend on the outline in its simplest ABA form remaining at the back of the listener's mind. It would take much space to list the modifications, great and small (and the small ones can be the most telling), that Handel introduces into the da capo aria. The majority have one vital element in common: they are inspired and controlled by the dramatic context—the words of the libretto and the emotional predicament of the character who sings them. Apart from the accompanied recitative, this was the sphere in which a composer of dramatic bent could find most scope.

It cannot be claimed that Handel originated all these variants of da capo design. If we knew what operas he heard, especially during his Italian years 1706–1710, and what scores he read (for although operas were seldom published they were often copied in manuscript), it might be possible to demonstrate what he owed to other composers and what was new. But it is quite likely that the search would be unrewarding. We might be forced to the conclusion that the sole novelty in Handel's opera arias was their genius: on the one hand the quality of his invention, on the other his ability to use a borrowed or commonplace formula to achieve an exceptional effect. While nearly all great artists possess this faculty, it lies at the heart of Handel's creative procedure. The most significant thing about his countless borrowings, whether from himself or others, is the unexpected light he throws on the old material. He was in one sense a great inventor; but he was equally a great adapter, improviser, and reconciler. That his treatment of da capo form was sometimes anticipated by Alessandro Scarlatti or Giovanni Bononcini or others (some of the modifications are found as early as *Almira*, when he was certainly following models) is not the point. What matters is the way Handel can set our blood on fire by the way he uses a device employed repeatedly by many composers before and since, including himself on occasion, without making any impression at all. Like Gluck and Mozart, he was a supreme master of the cliché.

The more closely we examine the da capo aria in Handel, the more flexible and less stereotyped it appears. Take for instance the opening ritornello. More often than not this prefigures the first phrase or melody sung by the voice. But the voice may treat it differently or introduce something new, which can be contrasted or combined with the ritornello.[3] In arias expressing emotional conflict the ritornello may present ideas of dissimilar or seemingly incompatible type, sometimes with a change of tempo or rhythm, and the voice may develop one, both, or neither of them.[4] There is no knowing in advance at what stage, if ever, the voice will take up any of the ideas of the ritornello, which may of course be suited only to instrumental treatment. Handel's delight, and ours, consists in a perpetual teasing and baffling of the expectation of the ear. One simple but unfailingly effective stroke is to make the voice overlap the ritornello by entering, perhaps with a sustained note, before the completion of its cadence. Asteria's aria at the end of Act II of *Tamerlano* and "O rendetemi" at the end of Act I of *Amadigi* are examples. This can become a positive element in the characterization, as happens with Bajazet's arias in *Tamerlano*. Not one of them waits for the cadence, and three—"Forte e lieto a morte andrei," "Ciel e terra armi di sdegno," and "Empio, per farti guerra"—begin with an emphatic word that calls forth its own gesture, followed by a rest.

Sometimes the ritornello is omitted or postponed. If the aria represents an immediate reaction to a question or a threat, it may interrupt the recitative cadence. Instead of waiting for the orchestra the voice enters at once, to suggest urgency or indignation. The ritornello may follow when the singer pauses for breath, or it may be withheld till the da capo, when it will alter the balance of the aria. A suppressed ritornello can convey gentler emotions. A particularly beautiful example from Handel's youth, Esilena's "Egli è tuo!" in *Rodrigo*, has been quoted above (example 12, p. 72); her entry without a pause brings home the spontaneous generosity of her offer to give up her husband if this will save the country from war. In examples 9 and 10 (pp. 65–67) the same stroke emphasizes directly opposite moods, of submission

---

[3] This plan was to reach its highest degree of refinement in the first movements of Mozart's piano concertos, which stem directly from the opera seria aria.

[4] See example 23 (p. 110), where the voice ignores both ritornello themes, and example 30 (p. 160), where it adopts one and ignores the other. In example 14 (pp. 84–85) it begins with a new idea and goes on to develop the second strain of the ritornello, leaving the first to the orchestra.

and rebellion, with equal appropriateness.[5] Episodes like this, which occur in every opera, refute the contention stressed even by Eisenschmidt that Handel's operas are no more than a succession of eloquent moments without psychological continuity, with the action halted for each aria and the ritornello raising a barrier against the rest of the scene.

The ritornello after the first part tends to balance or repeat the opening; but it can modify, extend, contract, or develop it. The whole design of Rosimonda's aria "Sì l'intendesti" in *Faramondo* expresses her sense of outrage when an unwelcome suitor pays court to her and she learns that her father has put him up to it, demanding the head of the man she loves in return. The opening ritornello consists of three bars very lightly scored; that at the end of the first part is sixteen bars long, built on material introduced by the voice and associated with Rosimonda's growing indignation, which exceeds her utterance and overflows into the orchestra. Lisaura's "Che tirannia d'amor!" in *Alessandro*, a tormented confession of reluctant love in F minor, has a ritornello that settles firmly in the dominant, C major, and the voice has to struggle to bring back the tonic. In the subsequent ritornellos the orchestra develops the material so freely that at the da capo the voice's opening phrase is modified, assuming a form reached in the ritornello after the first half. Alcina's "Ah! mio cor," with a ritornello on fresh material after the first half and none at all at the da capo, is a supreme instance of a complex emotional situation projected with the utmost force and clarity by a simple adjustment of the formal balance.[6]

Fulvia's aria of gentle reproach to her brutal father Massimo in *Ezio*, "Caro padre," is enriched in the lead back to the da capo by a Neapolitan sixth progression that has not occurred in the original ritornello; it takes up a similar chord in the second part, at the words "rimorso del tuo cor," and intensifies the impact of the da capo. The same opera has an example of the opposite process, subtraction instead of addition, in Massimo's "Tergi l'ingiuste lagrime," a sycophantic appeal

---

[5] Compare the treatment of ritornellos in the last scene of Act II of *Tamerlano*, p. 146 above.

[6] See examples 2–4, pp. 44–46; also example 14, pp. 84–85, which has many points of similarity.

to the daughter he has estranged. The main ritornello presents two
contradictory ideas, one smooth and lyrical, the other a chromatic
figure on the violins, pianissimo e staccato (example 30). The voice
makes its honeyed plea in terms of the first. The second is confined
to the orchestra and never reappears in its original form, though its
shadow lurks several times in the background; it clearly indicates the
cloven hoof. The second part of the aria shifts restlessly through a
series of minor keys, but when it leads back to the renewal of Massimo's
appeal in the da capo the chromatic figure is surprisingly omitted. For
a moment this almost steals our sympathy; but the sinister shadow resumes its place, and we know that this evil character, who has at-
tempted a treacherous murder and put the blame on Fulvia's innocent
lover, deserves neither her sympathy nor ours.[7] This aria leads to the
emotional climax of the opera, Fulvia's tragic scena "Misera, dove son?"

Example 30

[7] Handel employs a similar ritornello design for a tragic purpose in Arianna's
aria "Mio dolce amato sposo" at the end of Act I of *Giustino*.

of which Mozart was to compose a notable setting. Handel's aria, "Ah! non son io che parlo," is based on a group of simple but widely contrasted ideas, presented in bare juxtaposition in the ritornello but beautifully worked out and combined later.

Introduction of new material or reshaping of old can occur at any stage of the aria, in the voice or the orchestra, even in a final coda, where the ritornello after the da capo may differ completely from that after the first part. By prolonging the phrase-lengths or enriching the orchestration, or both, Handel produces an effect of sudden emotional intensity. The aria "Hò un non sò che nel cor," mentioned above, illustrates this procedure at its simplest. Arias with continuo accompaniment, especially in the early operas, sometimes have an extended coda for full orchestra with the original bass elevated to the treble and new parts added beneath. This type of design can be highly dramatic. Orlando in his madness sings an aria in B flat in gavotte rhythm, "Già lo stringo" (see example 31). In the first part, in bare octaves throughout, he imagines he is challenging Mars to mortal combat. In the second part the tempo changes to largo and he believes himself dead, killed by his own guilt; it is scored for string quartet without double bass or harpsichord and goes through a remarkable series of modulations, beginning in F minor and passing through A flat minor to C minor. Orlando's courage then returns, and he sings the da capo. But the coda, fully scored, introduces a variation of the melody in a new triplet rhythm, intended perhaps to suggest his sauntering exit in search of new adventures. The effect is redoubled by the fact that this is the only ritornello in the aria. The peculiarity of the design reflects the crazy recklessness of Orlando's conduct.

This is an extension of the method by which Handel builds up his melodic paragraphs. There is an equally striking example—a duet this time, not an aria—in Act III of *Arminio*, where Arminio's wife and sister proclaim it their duty to rescue or avenge him before resorting to suicide. This is a long arioso in which the material is never repeated but continues to throw off new offshoots up to the end of the coda. It conveys most vividly the mingled resolution and desperation of the two women. Some of these developments in the course of a movement seem to have been set off by a secondary idea seizing Han-

Example 31

2. Ritornello.

del's imagination as he wrote: for instance, the trills introduced towards the end of the first part of "Benchè povera donzella" in *Flavio*, which persist through its final ritornello and the second part, and the dotted figure treated similarly in the great B flat minor aria "Amor, nel mio penar" in the same opera.

Many surprises spring from a manipulation of tonality that may look negligible or obvious on paper. In the aria "Non disperi peregrino" at the end of Act II of *Lotario*, Handel moves from the tonic, E flat, into the dominant, but in such a devious manner, with feints into F minor and G minor, that he creates a sense of bold harmonic adventure, intensified later by a glimpse of E flat minor at the end of the first part. The sinfonia at the beginning of Act II of *Poro* illustrates another method of reaching the dominant by the backstairs. The aria in *Ariodante* in which Ginevra, condemned to death by her father, kisses his hand for what she thinks is the last time begins with a slow tragic theme in unison. We hear no harmony until the middle of the first part, when a pianissimo chord of the Neapolitan sixth strikes straight to the heart. A simple juxtaposition may be enough. Another tragic aria, Alcina's "Mi restano le lagrime" in F sharp minor, has a second part beginning in the illusory comfort of the tonic major, but it ends in G sharp minor, from which it drops back to F sharp minor for the da capo with an effect of increased desolation. The aria "Risolvo abbandonar" in Act II of *Alessandro,* in which Alexander decides to abandon love, an activity that has brought him singularly little success, and resume his military career, begins with an emphatic "No!" before the ritornello. The recitative cadence is in A major, but Alexander's "No!" (a word not in the libretto) is sung to an F natural, which becomes the tonic of the aria. The same progression occurs in Act I of *Rodelinda*, where Eduige resolves to punish the faithless Grimoaldo by offering herself to Garibaldo. In answer to Garibaldo's question, a recitative cadence in A major, she sings the first phrase of her aria, before the ritornello, in F major: "Lo farò"—"I will do it"—and the change of key brings out the abruptness of her decision.

Normally the first ritornello does not modulate far, if at all. It may hint at a modulation that occurs later in the aria; or more memorably it may feint one way, and when the voice reaches the corresponding point it may lead off in a different direction. The ritornello of "Del debellar la gloria" in *Scipione* produces an almost Mozartian flavor by moving from G major into A minor and back, anticipating a stroke in the aria. In *Radamisto's* "Ferite, uccidite" the ritornello sideslips from A major into a unison passage of ambiguous tonality with a leaning toward A minor; at the relevant point in the aria, on the words "che forza a penare il misero cor," Handel startles the ear with a plunge from A major into C major, changing the key signature for fifteen bars. Ezio, unjustly accused of treachery to the Emperor, surrenders his sword but thinks of the grief his disgrace will bring to Fulvia, who loves him. The first part of his aria "Recagli quell' acciaro" is in E flat, the upper instruments for much of the time in unison with the voice; the second part, abjuring the relative minor that everything has led us to expect, goes straight into C *major* ("E tu serena il ciglio") with a rich accompaniment in flowing semiquavers from the strings. We might be in the world of Schubert.

These modulations up or down a third, major or minor, are of course characteristic of the early romantic period. When Handel uses them, unprepared, to make a dramatic point, they have a powerful emotional impact that inevitably strikes us as romantic. He sets up a similar association when he slips quietly into the minor just before a final cadence, or ends a major key aria in the tonic minor. In *Atalanta* the heroine finds the lover she has been trying to resist asleep and calls down sweet dreams to comfort him. The unexpected change from A major to A minor for the last two bars of her arioso gives away her secret. He wakes up, and the scene continues in recitative. Arsamene's arioso "Per dar fine alla mia pena" in Act II of *Serse* likewise drops from G major to G minor in the closing bars as if reflecting his despair at losing Romilda. Serse tells him to cheer up: he can have his girl. Arsamene takes this as a bitter jest, especially when Serse offers him the wrong sister. He stoutly demands Romilda, plunging without ritornello into a second aria, "Sì, la voglio," full of expressive coloratura and once more in G major. This is another instance of the cavatina-cabaletta form, unified by tonality.

Occasionally, in defiance of the exit convention, two da capo arias are yoked like this. In Act II of *Arminio* the hero, chained and guarded,

sings a gloomily defiant aria ("Duri lacci!") in F minor.[8] His father-in-
law Segeste, a German who has gone over to the Romans, urges him
to make his submission. Arminio scornfully refuses: he would rather
die; it is Segeste who will be tortured by remorse. He goes out with a
brilliant aria in F major propelled by whiplash rhythms, the first two
words—"Sì, cadrò"—ejaculated before the ritornello. The two arias
are as contrasted in mood and texture as they are related in key.

The same act illustrates another aspect of Handel's control of
tonality, the unexpected use of the major mode where the emotional
content would seem to point to the minor. It ends with two consecutive
arias of this type. In the first the condemned Arminio entrusts his wife
Tusnelda to his enemy, the Roman general Varo, an honorable man
whom he knows to be in love with her; in the second Tusnelda begs
Varo to win her everlasting gratitude by sparing Arminio's life. Both
are slow arias relying not at all on vocal display, but a good deal on
harmonic suggestion. The choice of mode enables Handel to play the
tonality against the dramatic situation, and in Arminio's "Vado a morir,"
which is in E flat, to darken it with shadows of F minor and E flat
minor. Once more manipulation of the ritornellos plays a prominent
part. The E flat minor passage comes in the orchestra just before the
second part; the return from this to the da capo is foreshortened in
span (with the first phrase of the voice transferred to the violins) and
enriched in texture.

There may be abrupt contrasts in mood, rhythm, tempo, and orchestration between the two parts of the aria, or in one of them, or in
both. This can produce a design that sounds complex to the ear, though
it is still a da capo aria. If the first part has two opposed strains, AB,
and the second develops A or B, the result is either ABAAB or ABBAB,
both sounding very different from ABA—especially if the ritornellos of
the first half are modified in the da capo. "Deggio dunque" in Act III of
Radamisto is a fine example of this. The scheme is

<hr>

[8] The design of this aria does its best to disguise the da capo framework and
suggest a continuous development. Every ritornello takes a different course; that at
the end of the first part modulates to C minor before the second part (and therefore has to be changed after the da capo); there is none after the second part; and
the opening never returns except as an accompaniment to the voice.

First part {
  A. Adagio with cello obbligato* and bass; 3 bars ritornello, 5 bars with voice.
  B. Allegro with 2 oboes and 4-part strings; 12 bars with voice, 7 bars ritornello.
}

Second part   Adagio, scored as A and thematically related; 6 bars with voice, shortened two-bar ritornello leading back to the vocal entry in A, followed by regular da capo.

* Handel later rewrote the aria for soprano (in place of alto), substituting an oboe for a cello obbligato.

The first part can have its own middle section, in which case the result is ABACABA, a hint of the classical rondo form, or a closer-knit design like ABABABA. Nor does this exhaust the possibilities. When Handel employs a second tempo within the first part, often a few slow bars in a different time at the entry of the voice, he is apt to bring it back at unpredictable intervals and to expand or abbreviate it without notice. Berenice's "Chi t'intende?" a passionate address to the god of love, has three different tempi (Adagio, Andante, Andante allegro) in irregular alternation throughout the first part and a fourth (Andante larghetto) in the second. This aria, like "Deggio dunque," has a prominent obbligato part—for solo oboe.[9]

Not all Handel's arias are in da capo form. There are a few short binary pieces, with or without repeats; occasionally, as in Act II of *Tamerlano*,[10] Handel gives them an important structural function. Rondos are rarer, but nearly always of outstanding quality. It is only necessary to mention "Verdi prati" in *Alcina*, "Vaghe pupille" in *Orlando*, with its clinching final return to the theme in the coda, and Sosarme's very beautiful "In mille dolci modi"; this too has its musical climax in the coda, where the violins soar to an unexpected top D in the fourth bar of the fourteen-bar melody. Handel's last opera, *Deidamia*, contains an aria, "M'ai resa infelice," that approaches sonata form, though without development. The two subjects are contrasted in mood, rhythm, and tempo; the second is stated in the relative major and recapitulated in the tonic, G minor. The librettist introduces a neat

[9] The varied ritornellos are again worth study, especially the return after the second part.
[10] See p. 145 above.

type of historical irony here, for Deidamia is cursing Ulysses for spoiling her love affair with Achilles by summoning him to Troy, and she invokes raging tempests to prevent his return to Ithaca. We are meant to apply our knowledge of the different fates in store for Achilles and Ulysses, the one killed at Troy, the other condemned to ten years' wandering on the way home.

Handel gives little countenance to the textbook injunctions, quoted by some theorists, that the various types of opera seria aria (pathetic, bravura, and so on) must occur in regular rotation, and in particular that no character can sing two arias in succession. This seems to have been one of Metastasio's artificial reforms. Handel observes it in his Metastasio operas, but breaks away from it elsewhere, in earlier and later works. Another bogus convention fathered on opera seria is the idea that composers clung to terraced dynamics and never employed a crescendo or diminuendo. Handel used both throughout his career, from the early Italian years to the late oratorios. The aria "Chi vive amante" in *Poro* has a carefully marked crescendo in the opening ritornello, from piano through poco a poco più forte, up to forte, on a phrase later associated with the sighs of love.[11] We even find exceptions to the rule that a scene must end with a full aria or duet; but the occasional closing ariosos, such as "Nè men con l'ombre" and "Del mio caro Bacco" in *Serse*, are doubtless a throwback to the practice of the seventeenth century.

There is a special type of aria in which the singer addresses two other characters alternately, either phrase by phrase (as in "Empio, perverso cor!" in *Radamisto*, where Zenobia defies Tiridate Ardito e forte while reassuring her disguised husband Adagio e piano) or turning from one to the other in the second part. *Alcina* is rich in arias addressed to two characters, or in two contrasted tempi, or uttered partly as an ironic aside. *Faramondo* has one astonishing aria, "Voglia che sia," in which the hero resolves to kill a tyrant but hesitates when he remembers that his victim is the father of the girl he loves. The voice stops in the middle of a phrase, and the turmoil in his mind is expressed by the orchestra in a wild chromatic ritornello, a procedure more typical of Wagner than of the eighteenth century.

[11] There are similar crescendos in "Cor di padre" in Act III of *Tamerlano*.

In this instance the aria is resumed; elsewhere the break is final. As early as *Rodrigo* a beautiful slow aria ("Sommi Dei!") is terminated by a summons to arms at the most unexpected moment, when the singer has just settled into his relative key for the second part. The interruption of the duet "Prendi da questa mano" in *Ariodante*, placed with equal skill though very different in effect, occurs at the start of the da capo.[12] Toward the end of *Tolomeo* the hero drinks what he believes to be poison (it is in fact a sleeping draught) and collapses in the middle of an aria, in the middle of a sentence, and on an unresolved chord; the orchestra is left to restore the tonic. Amadigi faints in the middle of a word (in recitative) and has an aria cut off by magic.[13] *Orlando* once more offers an outstanding example. The hero, restored to sanity but believing he has killed Angelica and Medoro, resolves on suicide. This happens in an aria, which is interrupted in mid-course by a multiple surprise: he is about to throw himself over a cliff when Angelica enters and in an unforgettable phrase tells him to live (example 32, p. 170).

Handel often fuses aria and recitative, either by running one into the other without a cadence or by incorporating stretches of recitative within the aria structure. Sometimes this is all sung by the same character, as in Atalanta's "Sì, sì, mio ben" in *Serse* or the elaborate scena "Dall' ondoso periglio" in *Giulio Cesare*, where the accompanied recitative returns in the middle of the aria and the whole design is bound together by thematic reminiscence. Sometimes another character interposes a recitative between the second part and the da capo, as when Caesar cries out (as well he might) at the beauty of Cleopatra's "V'adoro pupille," or Eduige in *Rodelinda*, during Bertarido's "Con rauco mormorio," recognizes the voice of the brother she believed dead. Elmira's magnificent B flat minor aria "Notte cara" in *Floridante* has an accompanied recitative for its second part. She is waiting in her room at night to elope with her lover when she hears footsteps and imagines him approaching: the aria stops, and she breaks into excited recitative; but the footsteps fade away and she resumes the aria.

Rodelinda has two scenes, for Rodelinda herself in the cemetery in Act I and for Bertarido in prison in Act III, that (like Amadigi's "Notte

---

[12] See example 22, p. 105 above.
[13] See example 16, p. 88, also p. 136 above.

Example 32

amica" in Melissa's garden) begin as arioso and drop first into accompanied recitative, then into secco, carrying the action forward without check. The first of these is preceded by an example of the opposite process, an accompanied recitative that becomes an aria before we realize it. Bertarido, who has been reported dead, returns in disguise to the cypress grove containing the monuments of the kings of Lombardy. After gloomy reflections on the empty pageantry of death he reads the inscription on his own tomb and wonders what has become of his wife (example 33, p. 172).

A surprisingly large number of Handel's operas contain scenes in which the recitative-aria alternation breaks down and the music runs continuously for several movements. In this feature Handel may have been ahead of his contemporaries. His care for dramatic values led him to modify the formal scheme to express not only states of mind but character in action; and here most of all the stiffness of the convention enabled him to bring off all manner of surprises. This begins very early in his career. There is nothing tentative about the garden scene for Poppea and Ottone in *Agrippina*.[14] The climax of *Il Pastor Fido*, an opera scarcely remarkable for the tautness of its plot, is a duet of farewell for two lovers, one of whom has been condemned to death on a false charge of adultery. The duet leads without a break into an orchestral symphony as the priests make a solemn entry to claim their victim, and this in turn, by means of an abrupt progression, to an arioso for the High Priest, ordering the sacrifice to stop. Then at last there is some recitative explaining why he takes this course, after which he repeats his arioso, extending the scene and producing another variant of da capo form. The repeat was a refinement of Handel's; it is not in the libretto.

This running-on is particularly common in supernatural scenes. At the close of *Teseo* Medea's arioso leads into Minerva's accompanied recitative,[15] which introduces the coro. In Act II of *Silla* the dictator sings an arioso, accompanied by violins and recorders in double thirds, begging solace from the god of sleep. He closes his eyes, and we witness his dream, which follows without a pause. An unnamed but far

[14] See p. 109 above.
[15] See example 15, pp. 86–87 above.

Example 33

from peaceful deity[16] descends in a chariot drawn by two dragons and
surrounded by Furies carrying lighted torches, and sings a bloodthirsty
aria encouraging Silla to slaughter his enemies and dominate Rome by
force. Its second part is again an accompanied recitative. At the end of
the da capo, as the vision fades, Silla wakes up, wildly repeating the
first bars of the god's aria, and orders his assassins to begin slaughtering
a crowd of refugees in a temple, which they proceed to do.

In *Arianna* Theseus goes to sleep before his encounter with the
Minotaur. "Sleep in the Form of a venerable old Man on a Cloud" appears in person and orders the dreams (presumably dancers) to show
Theseus his future glory. They enact the coming fight, and he wakes
up with a start. Handel combines four movements, an arioso and three
accompanied recitatives, in a firm sequence united by tonal relationship
and a recurring motive in the orchestra; and the music runs on into
the next secco. When Theseus does meet the Minotaur in Act III
Handel rises to the occasion. Theseus sings a slow accompanied recitative in G minor and a fiery aria in E flat of great rhythmic power and
flexibility. Its final ritornello, after the da capo, is developed to more
than twice the original length as Theseus fights with and slays the
monster, and after a recitative in which he proclaims his triumph it is
repeated for his exit. Handel had repeated a ritornello in this manner
as early as *Almira*, but with far less effect. Theseus, as he goes off,
seems to be recalling the fight in his mind.

The dream scene in Act I of *Giustino* has a more varied scheme:
six movements (running to 286 bars) without the intervention of secco
recitative, and only the last of them in da capo form. Giustino goes
to sleep while plowing up an orchard and sees a vision of the goddess
Fortune, who descends sitting on a wheel in a grand machine attended
by genii. She encourages him to abandon the plow and conquer the
Byzantine Empire; her words are echoed by the genii in chorus, and
he accepts the task with enthusiasm. Handel unifies the design by a
method he had employed in the oratorio *Athalia*. Fortune enters to a
ritornello of twenty bars based on a rhythmic ostinato so vividly suggesting the rotation of a wheel as almost to evoke a picture of the

---

[16] He is called Astagorre in an autograph fragment in the Fitzwilliam Museum.

Example 34

goddess mounted on a bicycle (example 34, pp. 174–175). She sings an arioso built on this material, and an accompanied recitative in which she instructs Giustino. The chorus follows without ritornello, completing a free da capo design with a richer development of the arioso music. It ends with a long orchestral diminuendo, still on the wheel motive, as the dream fades and the instruments gradually drop out until first violins and string basses in pianissimo octaves are left. So far the whole scene has been in closely related flat keys. When Fortune and the genii vanish in B flat, Giustino welcomes his destiny in an accompanied recitative beginning on a first inversion of C major, and ends the scene with a full da capo aria in D major. The layout and the tonality are governed by the course of the drama, which they signally reinforce.

In the second-act garden scenes of *Alessandro* and *Tolomeo*, as well as *Agrippina*, the da capo scheme disintegrates as the result of intervention from other characters, but the ear's expectation of the da capo that never comes remains a valid force. Seleuce's aria "Dite che fà" in *Tolomeo* does end with a brief reference to the first part, but in the wrong key and sung by the wrong character. The *Alessandro* scene illustrates a point touched on in connection with *Poro*,[17] the ironical quotation by one character of music first sung by another. Alexander pays court to Rossane and Lisaura in turn, addressing each in a short arioso, unaware that on both occasions the other lady has been listening; each then makes him thoroughly uncomfortable by quoting back to him, in a different key, the arioso he addressed to her rival.

Several of Handel's operas show a primitive leitmotive technique, or at least the recall of earlier music to make a dramatic point. This may be ironical, as in *Alessandro, Poro,* and the jealousy duet in Act III of *Serse,* or structural, as in the *Arianna* and *Giustino* dream scenes. In the prison scene of *Silla* Flavia repeats the *second* part of an aria (in which she finds the prospect of life without her husband intolerable) with renewed pathos after a recitative in which Silla throws her husband's bloodstained cloak at her feet. Costanza's arioso at the beginning of Act II of *Riccardo Primo* returns in a different key as a symbol of her continuing unhappiness. When Rosmene pretends to be mad in Act III of *Imeneo,* her two lovers one after the other beg her to take their lives.

[17] See p. 141 above.

They do so to the same music, the arioso "Se la mia pace," which they presently repeat in extended form as a duet. The effect here is both ironical and structural—and very funny in the theater.

In *Serse* two short arias without initial ritornellos are repeated in their entirety with different words, one by a second character putting his own slant on the sentiments of the first, the other most amusingly by the same character to support a flagrant untruth. In Act I Serse orders his brother Arsamene to tell Romilda that he (Serse) loves her; when Arsamene refuses, he says he will tell her himself ("Io le dirò che l'amo") and goes out. Arsamene, to the same music, expresses his own confidence in her love ("Tu le dirai che l'ami, mà non t'ascolterà"). In Act II Atalanta tells Serse that Arsamene is in love with her and not with Romilda. The king is incredulous but delighted. Atalanta is careful to warn him, twice over, that Arsamene will deny it. Both episodes have a delicious tunefulness and lightness of touch.

It is customary to pass over the secco recitatives as mere links between the arias. This is to align ourselves with the prejudices of the contemporary audience rather than with the composer. While the function of the recitatives is inevitably subsidiary, and they bear occasional evidence of hasty composition, they are seldom as perfunctory as a first glance might suggest. In most of the mature operas their tonal structure is shaped with great care, as anyone who tries to cut them for performance soon discovers. To compare them unfavorably with the accompanied recitatives is beside the point, since the latter form was chosen to express moments of heightened tension, and therefore to stand out from the more level tone of secco.

In accompanied recitative Handel displays an imaginative range and a boldness in dramatic technique, tonality, elaboration, and design beyond any of his operatic contemporaries. Some of these pieces run to fifty bars or more, with numerous and unpredictable changes of meter, tempo, and dynamics; nearly every opera from 1720 on has at least one outstanding example. Broken rhythms, suspensions, and a rich crossing of the inner parts are common features. The scoring is not confined to strings. Bassoons appear in recitative in *Ottone,* drums and oboes in *Riccardo Primo,* trumpets and oboes in *Lotario,* recorders, oboes, bassoons, and a threefold division of the violins in *Alessandro.*

Handel seems to have taken a particular delight in exploring abstruse keys and remote, often enharmonic, modulations. "Alma del gran Pompeo" in *Giulio Cesare* begins in G sharp minor, changes its key signature in the middle of a bar, and ends enharmonically in A flat minor, followed by a secco recitative beginning in E major. Handel noted this progression in the autograph before setting any of the secco recitatives in the opera, one of many indications of careful tonal design. *Lotario* and *Ezio* also have accompanied recitatives in G sharp minor, while B flat minor, a favorite key for scenes of tragedy and despair, occurs in recitatives in *Almira, Scipione, Riccardo Primo, Siroe, Tolomeo,* and *Orlando,* and in many arias, especially during the Royal Academy period. *Rodelinda* has a long passage, almost an arioso, in F sharp major; *Ezio* a somber and chromatic scene, in a mood redolent of the Bach Passions, in E flat minor.

The bigger accompanied recitatives sometimes possess a thematic as well as a tonal unity. In "Chi vide mai più sventurato" (*Tamerlano*) and "O sventurati affetti" *(Scipione)* Handel creates a cyclic form by bringing back the initial phrase before leading into the aria. Elsewhere the drama takes control, and the music seems to break out of its period into the world of Gluck or even later composers. The beginning of Orlando's mad scene is one example. Another is Bajazet's suicide in Act III of *Tamerlano.* He has taken poison to cheat Tamerlano of his revenge, and enters at peace with himself for the first and only time in the opera. But he is soon convulsed with passion. He derides his conqueror, says an agonized farewell to his daughter, half regretting he has not taken her with him, invokes the Furies to torment Tamerlano's soul, and topples at last into incoherence. Handel links five accompanied recitatives, two ariosos, and a few bars of secco in a continuous stretch of music that reflects these moods with the aid of rapid changes of time and pace and passes through an astonishing range of keys and modulations, including one passage that begins in F sharp major and ends in E minor after spending most of the time in three flats (example 35). Bajazet's sudden collapse is very moving; the libretto directs him to utter the last broken syllables "as out of Breath" (example 36, pp. 180–181).

It is easy to appreciate, and difficult to exaggerate, the theatrical impact of such a scene. But Handel does not need to break the formal

Example 35

Example 36

sate! ahi_mè! se stan_che sie_te, la rab_bia mia prende_te,

o me_co lo por_ta_te là giù nel re_gno del fu_ror e_

(Và mancando nel ritirarsi dentro la scena, sostenuto sempre da Asteria ed Andronico.)

_ter_no! per tormen_tar, per la_ce_rar quel mostro, io sa___rò

la mag_gior fu_ria d'a_ver_no.

Example 37

va do ro, pu pil le, sa et te d'A mo re, le vo stre fa vil le son gra te nel sen,

le vo stre fa vil le son gra te nel sen.

mold. He can make a dramatic statement within the most orthodox da capo framework. Isolated from its context, the aria is still at least four things: a coherent musical unit, an outpouring of melody that generates its own continuations, the expression of a particular emotion or *Affekt,* and a vehicle for individual characterization. All four emerge clearly from Cleopatra's seduction aria in *Giulio Cesare,* with its vision of the Muses on Mount Parnassus. The tune is a miracle, and so is the instrumental texture, which employs two orchestras, one in the pit and one on the stage, including viola da gamba, theorbo, and harp. The forces are substantial, but they are treated with great delicacy; the violins in both orchestras are muted. This scene was designed to captivate the eye as well as the ear; while Cleopatra is aiming at Caesar's senses, Handel and his stage machinist are trying to ravish those of the audience. Most striking of all is the way Handel expresses Cleopatra's character and intentions through the vocal line, continually prolonging the melody by means of melismas and interrupted cadences, so that the first part of the aria is at once an indivisible musical paragraph and a portrait of the immortal harlot plying her trade (example 37, pp. 182–183).

CHAPTER 10

❦❦❦❦❦❦❦❦❦❦❦

Orchestration

Handel's treatment of the opera orchestra is another aspect of his art that calls for more attention that it has received. The orchestra is never a mere background or a cradle for the voice; it supplies the atmosphere in which the music breathes and through which it draws its life-blood. Three characteristics of Handel's practice may be singled out: the wide scope, both in choice of instruments and in their various blends and permutations; the intimate relationship with the dramatic context; and the feeling for timbre and texture, based on instinctive understanding of the instruments and an infallible ear. The first two, though perhaps not their full implications, are easily detected by the reader of the scores; the third can be very deceptive, a fact that must be held responsible for the astonishing amount of tasteless rescoring to which the music has been subjected.

Handel had an exceptional sensitivity to the balance of sound, whether instrumental, vocal, or mixed, and in particular to the exact spacing of chords, lines, and textures. He seems to have composed entirely for the ear, never filling up in order to complete a logical pattern, as one feels Bach sometimes did. Handel's music on paper can look thin, casual, and unsystematic. Of two consecutive pieces, one may exhibit the greatest care over nuances of instrumentation and dynamics while the second resembles a rough sketch without tempo or dynamic mark.[1] Yet the one may sound as magical as the other, and the fact of juxta-

---

[1] See example 40, p. 193 below, for an aria of this kind, where every note tells.

position can contribute to this. The arias with continuo only, in the mature operas at least, are always planned to convey an impression of intimacy suited to the context.

Taken as a whole, Handel's scoring is richer than that of his opera seria contemporaries (the charge of noisiness is proof of this) and may to some extent reflect the lasting influence of the Hamburg school, especially Keiser, who was fond of picturesque accompaniments. But it is again difficult in the present state of knowledge to say how much was new and how much borrowed. Handel has been credited with introducing horns into the opera house in *Radamisto;* this had been done five years earlier by Alessandro Scarlatti in *Tigrane* (1715) and possibly elsewhere. In opera and oratorio alike Handel did employ a wide range of instrumental color, even for an age when the orchestra was not standardized and obsolescent instruments like the theorbo and viola da gamba persisted alongside new inventions like the clarinet.

In his early years he must have been restricted by the instruments locally available and the skill of the players. The unidentified theater for which he composed *Rodrigo* possessed no brass. When Giuliano bids the trumpet sound to arms, it is the oboe that strikes up; Handel later adapted this aria ("Stragi, morti") for a new context in *Radamisto* and replaced the oboe with a trumpet. The most ample score of the Italian period, a treasury of sumptuous instrumental color, is the oratorio *La Resurrezione;* but this was composed for a specially assembled orchestra in a nobleman's palace, not for the public theater. Handel's delight in writing for such a body shines through the music. It was not so much the massive effects that excited him (this was to come later in the Coronation Anthems and some of the English oratorios) as the opportunity for combining and contrasting different textures, often of the utmost delicacy. The same is true of many of the London operas. Here he was well provided from the start (*Rinaldo* with its four trumpets was designed to make a splash), and for thirty years he led an orchestra renowned for its prowess. It included many of the leading players of the age, who no doubt appreciated Handel's qualities as much as he did theirs. Indeed, his reputation (if not his invitation) may have played a part in attracting them to London. The names of several—Kytch, the

Castrucci brothers, Giuseppe Sammartini, Caporale—appear in the auto-graphs against obbligato parts he composed for them.

The basis of his opera orchestra, as of all baroque orchestras, con-sisted of strings, oboes, bassoons, and harpsichord continuo. In three operas (*Siroe*, *Berenice*, and *Imeneo*) this is the complete band. Handel can produce striking effects with these limited forces, as in Berenice's aria "Chi t'intende?" where an elaborate oboe obbligato (probably written for Sammartini) is set off by warm four-part string harmony. This was a favorite layout, especially in a lyrical arioso at the beginning of a scene: "Quando mai spietata sorte" in *Radamisto*[2] is one of the loveliest examples (example 38, p. 188).

The employment of the same staves for violins and oboes is not a lazy or capricious device; nor is there anything automatic about the manner in which the instruments are doubled or detached. Countless variants are possible, and can be found in Handel's scores. When writing for both instruments he generally confines the oboes to the ritornellos, lightening the texture when the voice enters. But by no means always. In "Hai due vaghe pupillette" (*Silla*) it is the violins that are restricted to the ritornellos while the oboes accompany the voice. In "S'armi il fato" (*Teseo*) the oboes are silent until the ritornello after the first part, where they introduce new material.

One source of constant flexibility is of course the division of the baroque orchestra into concertino and ripieno groups, each with its own continuo. This is frequently specified in detail and probably occurred in all the operas, even (though on a reduced scale) in the one or two works like *Imeneo* where the orchestra was very small. It gave many oppor-tunities to the principal soloists, especially violin, cello, oboe, and bas-soon, and was a built-in safeguard against monotony. In particular the lightening of the bass in concertino passages, usually by the suppression of the double basses as well as the ripieno cellos and (except when the upper parts are taken by oboes) the bassoons prevented the heavy-footed-ness that is commonly, and erroneously, thought to be characteristic of the baroque orchestra. This is a much more widespread fault in nine-

---

[2] Compare also the ariosos "Dolce riposo" (p. 83 above) and "Chi ritorna" in *Teseo*.

Example 38

teenth-century music, and its intrusion into modern performances of Handel can be traced to a survival of "romantic" tradition. A stylish continuo player could, and can, aerate the whole score.

Handel was himself a violinist, and after his early years his writing for the instrument is seldom less than masterly. Like Bach, he can make an accompaniment of unison violins and continuo sound astonishingly full and sonorous; Bajazet's aria "A suoi piedi"[3] is an example. In scenes of longing or mental anguish demanding a concentrated intensity of expression (they are often accompanied recitatives) he draws a closely woven texture in which the upper and inner parts cross and intertwine, especially the two violins, or the second violin and viola, or all three.[4] There is an instance of his nice sense of balance (and quaint command of language) in Dorinda's arioso "Quando spieghi" in *Orlando*, where the top line in the ritornello is played by first violins "e 2 first seconds." He used mutes and pizzicato sparingly but with consummate effect. He liked a compound of muted upper strings and pizzicato basses, sometimes in combination with wind instruments—recorders in "Vaghe fonti" (*Agrippina*), bassoons in "Scherza infida" (*Ariodante*), both in the sinfonia in the opening scene of *Serse*[5]—but on occasion by themselves with the harpsichord silent. He seldom has all the strings muted or all pizzicato, though there are exceptions ("Occhi belli" in *Il Pastor Fido* and the second part of "Vo' far guerra" in *Rinaldo*, where they play pizzicato in octaves). He does sometimes contrast muted and unmuted upper strings, and pizzicato and arco basses, in the same piece: for example, the very lovely "Dite che fà" in the *Tolomeo* garden scene and Arsace's sleep aria "Mà quai note" in *Partenope*. In the latter the orchestra consists of two flutes, violins and violas muted, and a bass line for theorbo and pizzicato string basses, but no bassoons or harpsichord. When Rosmira enters, finds Arsace asleep, and is overcome by loving thoughts, her accompanied recitative has the upper strings still muted but the basses *con l'arco, mà piano*. Another exquisitely scored sleep aria

---

[3] Example 11, pp. 70–71 above.

[4] See p. 197 below and example 27, pp. 138–139 above.

[5] This episode, with its rustling double thirds and the suppression of the continuo in the whispered interjections of Arsamene and Elviro, is a marvel of delicacy and wit.

is Orlando's "Già l'ebro mio ciglio," accompanied by two violette marine (viole d'amore), played by the Castrucci brothers, and pizzicato basses. The same instruments may have been employed in Onoria's aria "Quanto mai felice siete" in *Ezio* (composed a few months earlier), which has a delightful accompaniment for two flutes, two violins, two violette, and bass. Handel does not always give the violas the scurvy treatment of which they like to complain; they are divided in a number of arias,[6] as are the cellos. Examples of both occur in *Teseo*. Several operas (*Agrippina, Radamisto, Alcina, Arianna*) have outstandingly beautiful arias with cello obbligato.

Nearly all Handel's operas contain parts for additional wind instruments. Treble recorders (flauto) occur in twenty-five, transverse flutes (traversa) in seventeen, both types of flute in eleven. They generally play in pairs, but there are a number of obbligato solos, especially for transverse flute. The recorders have more to do in the operas, of all dates, than the flutes; there is no question of the recorder becoming obsolete at this period, though it drops out in the later oratorios. To judge from the music he wrote for it, Handel had a special affection for its tone. He did not confine himself to the treble members of the flute family. Sopranino recorders (or possibly flageolets) appear in *Rinaldo, Riccardo Primo*, and *Alcina*, and a consort, including a bass, in *Giustino*. *Riccardo Primo* has an obbligato for traversa bassa, the alto flute in G; it is within the compass of the ordinary flute, but gains considerably from the more somber alto.

Flute and recorder parts were played by the same players, who were often oboists as well. Only in this sense are the parts interchangeable, for Handel used the two instruments in different contexts, the recorders mostly for pastoral and outdoor scenes, the flutes to suggest grief or mourning. His choice is always idiomatic, never fortuitous. The mocking, ironical effect of the treble recorders in Ruggiero's "Mio bel tesoro" in *Alcina* is lost if transverse flutes are substituted. Occasionally, for a special purpose, Handel introduced both instruments in the same piece, either doubled (the duet "Vivo in te" in *Tamerlano*) or independently (the second part of "Con rauco mormorio" in *Rodelinda*,

---

[6] In *Almira* they are sometimes used without the violins, alone or with recorders.

where a choir of two violins, divided violas, two recorders, one flute, and bassoons in various groupings express nature's echo of the singer's lament for his lost happiness).

There are obbligato parts for two cornetti in *Tamerlano* ("Par che mi nasca") and two clarinets (chaloumeaux) in *Riccardo Primo* ("Quando non vedo"), both slow arias of exceptional beauty. It is not certain that Handel used the instruments in performance, for he supplied alternative versions, with flutes in the one case and oboes in the other. (In the Granville copy of *Tamerlano* the cornetti are replaced by clarinets.) The bassoons are not confined to their regular service as bass support for the oboes. From time to time they double the voice in bass arias or enjoy an independent part or parts, adding great richness to the tenor register. In "Per tutto il timore" (*Ezio*) they double the violas or the bass in the first part, but break out into open country in the second. They make an unforgettable impression when contrasted in rhythm and note values with the rest of the orchestra: quicker in "Per tutto il timore," slower with lingering suspensions in "Se pietà" (*Giulio Cesare*) and "Scherza infida" (*Ariodante*), each in turn in "Pena tiranna" (*Amadigi*) (example 39, p. 192). The mood of these scenes is tragic or pastoral, never comic.

Handel wrote for brass instruments in thirty-one of the thirty-nine operas, and in revivals of at least one more (*Il Pastor Fido*), though horns are not found before the Royal Academy period. Thenceforth he often used trumpets and horns in the same opera, playing separately or—especially in the coro—together. *Giulio Cesare* has two pairs of horns in tonic and dominant keys (there appears to be no contemporary parallel for this) and the only aria in the operas with an obbligato for solo horn. Trumpet obbligatos are more common; there are examples in *Silla*, *Amadigi* (two), *Radamisto*, *Ezio*, and *Giustino*. In one aria in *Rinaldo*, a stirring battle piece for the castrato Nicolini, the voice has to compete with four trumpets; Handel takes care not to drown it.[7] Timpani are mentioned in six operas, but may have played with the trumpets in others. It is likely that side drums (*tamburi*), referred to in the stage directions of *Partenope*, accompanied military flourishes in the recitative.

[7] The aria can be—and in two recent revivals has been—sung with splendid effect by a woman.

Example 39

The libretto of *Almira* could be taken to justify the employment of a number of more exotic instruments that have no written parts in the score, including the bagpipes.

Example 40

These forces offered Handel almost unlimited opportunities for exploiting his mastery of the orchestral palette. He regularly employed instrumental color for emotional and dramatic expression, and he achieved some wonderful effects with different and ever shifting blends of string, woodwind, and brass tone. They vary in scale from the simple to the very elaborate. The old idea that a baroque composer did not care which instruments played the treble line does not apply to Handel. When he doubles the first violin with a flute, he has in mind a particular quality of sound. Examples are the pastoral siciliano "Mi volgo" in *Tolomeo*, Polissena's aria "Tu vuoi ch'io parta" in *Radamisto*,[8] and Cleopatra's "Piangerò la sorte mia" in *Giulio Cesare*, where the combination contributes enormously to the haunting character of the music. This quality is difficult to define in words: a mixture perhaps of plaintiveness, nostalgia, and self-indulgence. It disappears if the top line is played experimentally by flute or violins alone (example 40, p. 193). Elsewhere Handel doubles violins and recorders ("Cessa omai" in the same opera), flutes and recorders,[9] recorders and oboes (the duet "Quando più minaccia" in *Arminio*), recorders and a solo oboe, and viola and bass recorder.[10]

On a more sumptuous scale are the eight- and nine-part accompaniments of arias like "Qual leon" in *Arianna* (two horns, two oboes, bassoons, four-part strings) and "Senza procelle ancora" in *Poro* (two horns, two recorders, four-part strings), with their sonorous spacing and delightful echo and pedal effects (example 41). The last is a favorite combination in pastoral scenes, where it evokes a mood of lingering nostalgia comparable perhaps to that of Watteau's landscapes with figures. In Ezio's "Se la mia vita" Handel reinforces and contrasts this octet from time to time with divided bassoons and four string soloists, violin, viola, cello, and double bass; the constantly changing texture has a fascinating delicacy and unexpectedness. Rich scoring with Handel is not a substitute for invention in other fields. Indeed the same episodes are often as remarkable for melodic and harmonic as for instrumental resource, and the most original in dramatic or formal organization, as if the creative impulse were exerting an equally powerful force on all his

[8] Example 9, p. 65 above.
[9] See p. 190 above.
[10] The last two in the same piece; see p. 197 below.

Example 41

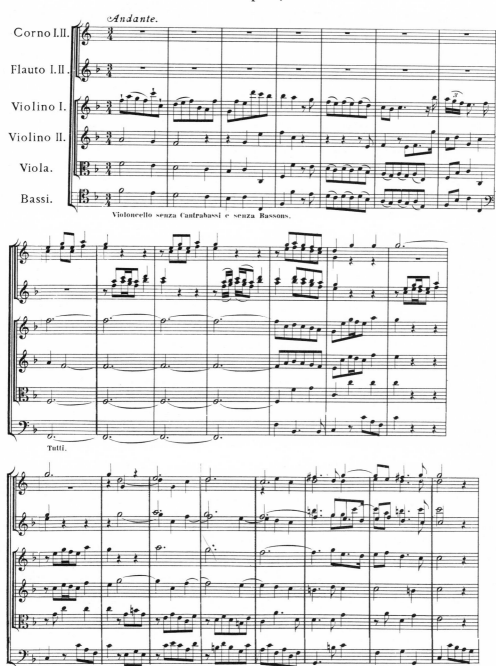

faculties. The Parnassus scene in *Giulio Cesare*[11] and the garden scene in *Tolomeo* are conspicuous examples. Compare too the bold and brilliant treatment of the ritornellos in "Senza procelle ancora" (before and after the first part), "Quando più minaccia," "Luci care" in *Admeto*, and "Quando può nascer" in *Giustino*.[12]

On at least three occasions—the Parnassus scene, the finale of *Ariodante*, and the first scene of *Deidamia*—Handel divided his orchestra physically, placing a second group (a substantial one in *Giulio Cesare*) on or behind the stage. He treated the two groups in combination and antiphonally, making a positive use of space in the old Venetian manner. This may have been a more frequent occurrence, for the librettos of *Almira* and *Giustino* refer to instrumentalists on the stage, and so does the autograph of *Poro*, where the sinfonia with horns in Act I is marked "le Corna [sic] di Caccia sul Teatro." In most if not all the operas there were two harpsichords, one for the concertini and one for the ripieni. The duet "Tu caro, caro sei" in *Sosarme* shows a slight but characteristic variant of this, the orchestra being split into two bodies, one supporting each singer. Elmira is accompanied by the violins and *Cembalo primo con i suoi Bassi*, Sosarme by four violas in unison and *Cembalo secondo colla Teorba, e i suoi Bassi*. When the voices sing together the groups combine, the bass line marked *Tutti, mà pp;* the oboes are silent except in the fore and aft ritornellos.

Other continuo instruments occur from time to time. *Giulio Cesare* has a harp and viola da gamba, sometimes with the parts written out, and a theorbo or bass lute appears in five operas, including the last, *Deidamia*. The organ is never mentioned in the operas, though there is one reference to it in the ballet *Terpsicore*, which served as a prologue to the November 1734 revival of *Il Pastor Fido*. This instrument is certainly not essential, as it is in the oratorio choruses, and could wreck a modern performance unless treated with the utmost discretion. There appears to be no evidence that Handel used an organ in the opera house before the memorable season of 1732, when he introduced oratorio to London.

A telling feature to which attention seems never to have been

[11] Example 37, pp. 182–183 above.
[12] See pp. 161 above and 197 below.

drawn is the deliberate withholding of one instrumental color until it can be brought in with the maximum effect, whether on a small time-scale in an aria or on an extended scale in the opera as a whole. "Luci care" in Act I of *Admeto*, where Alcestis resolves to die for her husband and looks forward to meeting him in the Elysian Fields, is a tragic F minor arioso of exceptional length (101 slow bars) and a superb piece of music by any standards; the crowning stroke is the unheralded entry of a single flute, the instrument of grief, at bar 45. This piece illustrates two points made earlier, the eloquent crossing of the string parts and the structural treatment of the ritornellos: six bars for continuo alone at the outset, but an intensely emotional coda of ten bars in five-part counterpoint for flute and strings. In the duet that ends Act II of *Faramondo* the flute enters at the octave with the second voice (Rosimonda's, when she offers Faramondo the consolation of hope);[13] it has been silent throughout the ritornello and the first vocal entry, and is never heard again in the opera. In Angelica's "Verdi piante" in *Orlando*, her farewell to the place where she and Medoro have enjoyed so much happiness (another piece with interwoven string parts), the recorders play only a few short phrases, not entering till bar 32, where they achieve a complete surprise. No one who has experienced this thrill is likely to forget it.

Perhaps the most astonishing stroke of this kind occurs in Giustino's arioso "Può ben nascer," his first utterance in the opera, before Fortune has summoned him to glory. This begins with an enormous ritornello of 44 larghetto bars, scored for two choirs of treble recorders, the first doubled by a solo oboe, and a bass recorder doubled by viola; no other strings and no continuo. When the voice enters, it is supported by two violins and bass, still without harpsichord; but the sixteen-bar coda is a blaze of color, bringing in, besides all the instruments heard hitherto, the full body of strings, the harpsichord, and two horns (their first appearance in the opera). The music does not repeat earlier material but continues to develop it in a surpassingly rich nine-part texture. There is no other instance of Handel introducing the horns for the first time in a vocal movement after the voice is silent.

He follows a similar method in the planning of a whole opera. In

13 See p. 141 above.

Rodelinda and *Faramondo*, and in the English drama *Hercules*, the horns are withheld till the final coro, when the dark web of conspiracy, suspicion, and vindictiveness has been dispelled. Handel has something in reserve for the festivities that could so easily be an anticlimax. In *Ariodante* he uses horns in Act I, but keeps the trumpets for the scene halfway through Act III in which Ginevra's honor is vindicated in the lists, just after she has resigned herself to execution. More remarkable perhaps is the treatment of the oboes in *Arminio*. These orchestral standbys double the violins in the overture and a symphony at the beginning of Act II, but do not appear at all in the vocal pieces till the brilliant aria "Quella fiamma" towards the end of the second act. This was a showpiece for the soprano castrato Conti and has three oboe parts, a spectacular obbligato for Giuseppe Sammartini and two ripieno parts as well.[14] It must have required some strength of mind to keep one of the most prominent instruments in the orchestra, and one of the finest players, so completely out of the picture until more than halfway through the opera. This restraint is abundantly justified in the event.

All this is part of Handel's technique of surprise,[15] and reveals his sensitivity to large-scale design—or maybe the need to supply a substitute for it. This can be seen on many levels;[16] the orchestral layout, for instance, is adjusted from the start to the background and temper of the libretto. *Il Pastor Fido* in its 1712 version is very lightly scored, whereas its predecessor, *Rinaldo*, has four trumpets and drums in the military scenes and three recorders for the birds. Other operas concerned with heroic warfare, like *Radamisto*, *Alessandro*, and *Riccardo Primo*, likewise concentrate on orchestral pageantry. In *Riccardo* Handel went

[14] A similar aria concludes Act II of the next opera, *Giustino*, but there is no question here of the oboes being held back for the occasion.

[15] Considerations of the same kind sometimes influenced his vocal writing. In *Ariodante* he deployed the full two-octave range of Carestini's voice only in his last aria, and then not till the end of the first part. The words of this aria, "Dopo notte atra e funesta," acclaiming the dawn of happiness after a night of black torment, are a paraphrase of the finale of *Tamerlano;* but where the latter context inspired a tragic setting in contradiction of the text, in *Ariodante* the mood is one of unclouded joy.

[16] Not only in the scoring: Polissena's final explosion in *Radamisto* (example 10, pp. 66–67 above) and many arias at the end of acts (see p. 140 above) owe their decisive impact to careful preparation in advance.

out of his way to celebrate George II's coronation and his own naturalization with the most splendid orchestra at his command, as the unique
sequence of wind obbligatos in Act III and the sumptuous texture of
the whole opera bear witness. Richard himself, standing for George II,
has a bravura aria accompanied by two trumpets, drums, oboes, and
complete string band, perhaps the most powerful body Senesino ever
had to contend with. The scoring of *Teseo* is almost as elaborate, but
totally different in effect, with the emphasis on delicacy and blended
colors rather than splendor. Seven instruments are used in pairs, including
violas and bassoons. There is a duet with the oboes and violas divided,
but the violins in unison, and an aria with recorders, violins, and violas
all in pairs.

In the successful early years of the Royal Academy Handel did not
always deploy his full resources. *Floridante* uses almost the same orchestra as *Radamisto,* though the texture (as befits the story) is much
lighter. But in the next two operas, *Ottone* and *Flavio,* he omits the brass,
as he does again in *Tamerlano,* a grand opera in its theme but one that
depends on character rather than incident or spectacle. Yet in *Giulio
Cesare* the same year he has four horns and a great deal else, and of the
nineteen operas following *Tamerlano* all but one have horns and more
than half have trumpets too. Even in *Deidamia,* produced when his fortunes were at a low ebb, he writes for substantial forces, including
trumpets and horns. His orchestra was never limited by his bank balance.
As when he composed a pair of utterly dissimilar works for the same
season—*Lotario* and *Partenope* for 1729–30, *Solomon* and *Susanna* for
1749—the governing factor was the dramatic content, and that alone.

CHAPTER 11

✤✤✤✤✤✤✤✤✤✤✤

Modern Revivals

The staging of Handel's operas in the modern theater presents a number of problems, great and small. They have usually been recognized, occasionally solved, sometimes shirked, and frequently exacerbated in the revivals of the last half century. There are also imaginary problems, which only appear as such because performers, audiences, critics, and scholars have misunderstood Handel, his period, and the nature of opera as an art. A glance at the history of these revivals may explain how this came about.

The movement began in Germany in 1920, when *Rodelinda* was produced at Göttingen. During the next ten years, fifteen of Handel's operas were staged in Germany, some in a dozen or more theaters with conspicuous success. The earliest productions were arranged and conducted by Oskar Hagen, whose versions were published in vocal score and can still be heard. A second wave of German revivals followed in the late 1930s and 1940s, and has since been extended by the annual festivals at Halle, Handel's birthplace, where it seems to be the intention to perform the entire cycle of his operas in rotation. Between 1920 and 1968 thirty-one of Handel's thirty-nine surviving operas have been revived on the stages of sixteen countries (including Finland, Spain, and Japan), twenty-eight of them in Germany, twenty in Britain, and seven in the United States. Apart from a few pre-war performances of *Giulio Cesare, Rodelinda,* and *Serse,* virtually all the non-German productions have taken place since 1955, the year in which the movement started in England with an almost accidental presentation of *Deidamia*.[1]

These revivals have had different aims and used very different means. The Hagen versions were heavily abridged and rewritten. The da capos were nearly all cut, and even the first parts of the arias chopped up and sometimes reduced to a fragment of ritornello. Many were omitted altogether. The accompaniments, including secco recitatives, were rescored for a romantic orchestra, no ornaments or appoggiaturas were admitted, and all male parts in the soprano and alto clefs, whether written for men or women, were put down an octave. It may be that some such measures were necessary to get the operas on the stage at all in 1920. Unfortunately they had the effect of starting the whole movement off on the wrong foot. They produced a hybrid, neither baroque nor romantic nor modern, but a little of everything. A performance of *Giulio Cesare* that sounds like nothing so much as a cross between the *St. Matthew Passion* and *The Flying Dutchman* does no lasting service to Handel. Although recent German revivals have seldom gone as far as this, Handel's image in Europe, especially Germany, is still saddled with a load of false tradition. This may well have contributed to the slowness with which his operas have won wider recognition, not because their texture has puzzled modern audiences, but because they have scarcely ever been allowed to hear it. The pernicious habit of octave transposition has even corrupted the texts of the new Halle complete edition, where parts composed for women may be found printed in the bass clef.[2] The fact that the Munich Opera to this day performs *Serse* in the Hagen version indicates the urgent need for radical rethinking.

The English revivals have avoided the worst pitfalls—rescoring and (in most cases) octave transposition—but have fallen into others, such as injudicious cutting. They have also begun to grapple with the question of ornaments and appoggiaturas. While the results have not always been convincing or consistent, this is a move in the right direction. A fully

---

[1] Edward J. Dent offered to translate this opera for Charles Farncombe and the Board of Trade Choir. The venture resulted in the foundation of the Handel Opera Society, which has since staged thirteen of Handel's dramatic works.

[2] For example, Valentiniano in *Ezio* and Polinesso in *Ariodante*.

ornamented (though partly rescored) version of *Agrippina*, edited by
Hellmuth Christian Wolff, has been performed and published in Germany; but it appears to be the policy at Halle to reject ornamentation,
which can be defended, and to accept rescoring and octave transposition,
which cannot.

It would be unfair to lay all the blame on the Germans. The position
is worse in Italy, to judge from the mangled and hideously defaced torso
to which the Piccola Scala reduced *Serse* in 1962. It is a depressing fact
that the most dismal experiences have been offered by professional or-
ganizations willing to lavish large sums on a spectacular production but
not to take a serious view of the music. Covent Garden has witnessed
two recent revivals of *Alcina*. That of the Stockholm Opera (1960)
looked well but was musically disastrous, not so much because Ruggiero
was sung by a baritone but because every aria except one was mutilated,
often leaving a meaningless fragment, and there was no room for the
score to breathe or express the drama. This may have been the old
German version produced at Leipzig in 1928 in the Hagen era; if so,
it should be dumped in the ocean with other waste products of our
civilized century. The second revival (1962), directed by Franco Zeffirelli and seen also in Venice and Dallas, preserved the pitch of the
voices but treated the drama with contempt by presenting it as a plot
within a plot, an entertainment put on as a diversion at some imaginary
baroque court. The prince and his courtiers (who of course have no
place in Handel's opera) remained on stage throughout; the singers
bowed to the prince after their arias, while the courtiers took care to
distract attention with irrelevant business. The ballet movements, introduced by Handel with masterly effect to crown two dramatic climaxes,
were distributed singly and at random between the arias, as if de-
liberately to destroy any vestige of tension or coherence.

In 1965 *Giulio Cesare* had its first professional stage production in
America, at Kansas City. This great opportunity was squandered, thanks
to a version that made nonsense of music and drama alike. There was
rescoring; there was wholesale transposition into the wrong octave; and
there was a novel method of solving the problem of length by the insertion of substantial slabs of other works into the most inappropriate

contexts.[3] The seduction scene in Act II, which might be described as a mixture of harlotry and politics, was padded out by the interpolation of the heartbroken farewell duet for the young lovers in Act III of *Tamerlano*. A fair parallel would be a performance of Verdi's *Otello* in which Desdemona begins the last act by firing off Lady Macbeth's sleep-walking scene.

In these three productions much time, energy, and money was spent on the visual element. No one could object to that; but what is the point of superimposing a spectacular scaffolding that flatly contradicts the music (as happened most conspicuously in the Zeffirelli *Alcina*) when the opera as Handel wrote it contains as many opportunities for the director, the choreographer, and the scene designer as the most ambitious individualist could desire? The staging of a Handel opera is a gift to the large modern opera house, provided the director takes the trouble to learn how the eighteenth-century theater worked (there is a fully equipped building with its original scenery at Drottningholm in Sweden) and resists the temptation to sacrifice the score to his own cleverness. He need not reject modern techniques; but he ought to apply them in the spirit of the period. If he is unwilling to do this, the conductor should take command and insist on the priority of the music. Often the most satisfactory revivals have been the work of universities and other partly amateur bodies who have lacked the money for elaborate staging and concentrated on an adequate interpretation of the score. That something is lost by abridgment of the spectacle cannot be doubted, especially in the magic operas. But if the musical performance is misconceived, no amount of pageantry can compensate for it.

It should be obvious that if Handel's operas are to give the full pleasure of which they are capable, they need to be approached with respect. To manhandle them into conformity with later styles not only saps their vitality; it attempts the impossible, since they belong to another age and can only speak, except under a crippling handicap, in terms of its convention. This is not a plea for the imitation of an eighteenth-

---

[3] See the long review in the London *Times*, May 24, 1965. The New York City Opera production of 1966, since recorded by RCA Victor, to a great extent followed the same deplorable policy.

century performance, which would be pedantic, or for literal subservi-
ence to the notes as written, which would be unhistorical. Strict authenticity in the antiquarian sense, even if it were desirable, is not practical. We should have to build and furnish theaters to reproduce the
acoustics of Handel's day, confine ourselves to eighteenth-century instruments, cultivate an eighteenth-century social sense—perhaps even an
eighteenth-century sense of smell—and organize a supply of castrati,
which appear to be among the few facilities not available at an American
university.

Baroque production technique was based on a stylized system of
ritual and gesture. To some extent this reflected the ceremonial of contemporary courts; the characters were expected to carry themselves like
persons of equivalent rank in society. The aim however was not natural-
istic illusion—far from it—but the representation of passion according
to the artistic conventions of the day. Eisenschmidt in an admirable
phrase calls Handel's operas timeless because perfectly in tune with their
time, whose theatrical compromises they employed as constructive material. He makes an urgent plea for the authentic touch. Unfortunately
he confines his argument to staging, scenery, and gesture, and does not
extend it to the music. The two aspects of course are intimately connected; again and again the music gives the clue to the gestures the composer had in mind. How literal we should be in adopting the stage movements and postures illustrated in contemporary manuals is debatable. But
we do need to discover what Handel was trying to do, how he achieved
it, and how this can be reconciled with modern resources.

The first problem to be faced is the matter of length. Most of
Handel's operas, if performed complete, would outlast the patience of
the modern listener. It is possible to envisage an audience going to
Handel as they go to Wagner, prepared to enjoy or endure for four
hours or more. But that time is not yet, and it is still necessary to cut.
On occasion Handel himself made cuts, generally of virtuoso vocal
passages, within the body of an aria, or omitted the second part and da
capo. This may have been a temporary measure enforced by a weak
singer; but it does little violence to the score provided it is not repeated
too often and provided the integrity of the da capo aria is respected.
That condition is not fulfilled if both parts of the aria are played but

the da capo confined to an instrumental ritornello. This allows all the vocal music to be heard (though not necessarily all the music, since a varied ritornello before or after the da capo may be lost) at the cost of unbalancing the aria and often the scene as well. Some of Handel's happiest surprises spring from the deliberate unbalancing of an occasional aria to make a dramatic point. If this is extended to other arias, the effect is weakened or lost.

It is sometimes possible to shorten the recitative, again following the precedent of the composer; but this needs care, for it can upset the tonal and the dramatic design. Both within the recitative and at the beginning of arias, especially those without initial ritornello, Handel likes to surprise us by implying one key and stating another. Nor does he always reveal in advance which character is to have the aria; it may not be the one who enjoys the last word in recitative. Here the surprise can follow the ritornello, when a different voice enters from the one we expect. Instead of many small cuts it may be less damaging to omit a whole aria or scene, where this can be done without mutilating the plot. Most operas have an occasional dramatically superfluous aria in which Handel has not been inspired by the character or the singer. But it may not be a simple matter to determine what is expendable, as the analysis of *Alcina* in chapter 4 above will have indicated.

It is inexcusable to cut a ritornello to facilitate the task of the director; he is there to produce what the composer wrote, not to rehash it for his own convenience. It is surprising how many directors fail to realize that the ritornello is an organic part of the design. Nor should da capo arias be abbreviated just because they are da capo arias, out of fear that repetitions are automatically boring. A da capo is not, or should not be, a mere repetition. Apart from Handel's resource in turning it to positive account, musically and dramatically, by adjusting the balance of the ritornellos, the tasteful use of ornament can enrich it to the advantage of the music and the listener as well as the singer.

Here we reach controversial ground. The bounds of good taste are not subject to strict definition, and there is something to be said for proceeding by trial and error; but it is possible to eliminate many errors in advance. A singer's ornaments are not a matter of unfettered license. They should be in the style of Handel's period, not that of Mozart or

Donizetti; should spring naturally from the vocal line, instead of distorting or supplanting it; should give the impression of being improvised, even if they are not. Ariosos and the first parts of arias need little or no decoration, apart from cadential trills and appoggiaturas. There can be no justification for embroidering a phrase at its first appearance, or for filling up an interval that gives character to the vocal line. Cadenzas should be short: Quantz insisted that cadenzas for wind must be delivered in a single breath, and the voice is a wind instrument.

These matters require emphasis, since the danger in some recent English revivals and recordings has been not too little ornament but too much, which can be equally ill-considered and a good deal more offensive. The pendulum has shown signs of swinging too far. Ornament, like salt, jades the palate if applied with too promiscuous a hand. Art has its law of diminishing returns. The singer or conductor who cannot leave well alone, like the director of similar inclination, becomes a parasite, drinking the blood of the music. The probability that this occurred from time to time in the eighteenth century makes a poor defense today.

The principal nonproblems likewise concern the singers. We are sometimes told that the vocal difficulties of baroque opera seria are insuperable, since modern singers are not trained to sing this type of music and we cannot produce a convincing substitute for the castrati. Both statements are untrue. It has been repeatedly demonstrated that the music is not beyond the capacity of modern singers, provided they take the trouble to study the idiom and are willing to use their intelligence as well as their throats. Some parts are more taxing than others; but Handel wrote for moderate as well as first-rate singers, especially in the later operas, and his vocal writing at its most formidable is no more arduous than much of Mozart or Rossini—not to mention what some modern composers feel impelled to inflict upon the voice.

The castrato difficulty has been magnified out of all proportion by ignorance and defective scholarship. Although we do not know exactly what the castrato voice sounded like, there are two valid substitutes, both of which were used by the composer. One is the countertenor. Handel wrote for only one countertenor in his operas, William Savage, who had the curious distinction of singing under him in all four clefs. In *Fara-*

mondo he combined the soprano role of Childerico with the tenor part in the final coro; later he was to achieve fame as a bass. Since Handel's opera company always included at least one castrato, and sometimes two or three, he had little need for countertenors, though he used them more frequently in the oratorios. Modern countertenors of sufficient quality are not thick on the ground, chiefly because this type of voice has seldom been required outside cathedral choirs; but there seems no reason why the demand should not stimulate the supply. That they can discharge the burden of Handel's music has been proved by the performance of singers like Russell Oberlin and Alfred Deller.

The second substitute for the castrato is the female voice of equivalent pitch. This was Handel's regular resource when he did not have enough castrati, and even when he did he sometimes preferred to give the male lead to a woman, as in the first version of *Radamisto*. His treatment of the voices in revivals, the evidence for which seems never to have been collected, is significant in this connection. It often happened, when he wished to revive an opera, that his company contained a different distribution of voices from the original cast. This necessitated various types of alteration and transposition, which follow definite patterns. He not infrequently transposed soprano parts for alto and tenor parts for bass, and occasionally, four or five times in all, alto parts for tenor. This meant a change in pitch of anything from a tone to a fourth or fifth. What we scarcely ever find is transposition by an octave. At first glance this would appear much the easiest course, saving the trouble of rewriting the orchestral parts to keep them within the compass of the instruments: the voice goes down an octave and the rest stands. Yet Handel goes to an immense expenditure of effort to avoid this, especially in alto parts. This cannot be dismissed as caprice.

Most of his leading castrati throughout his career—Nicolini, Valentini, Senesino, Berenstadt, Pacini, Baldi, Bernacchi, Carestini, Annibali—were altos or mezzo-sopranos. Of the sixty castrato roles in his operas as originally composed, forty-five, including nearly all the biggest, are for alto voice. In revivals where no alto castrato was available they were taken generally by women contraltos, occasionally by sopranos or tenors. There is not one confirmed instance of an alto castrato part, or

even an aria, being put down an octave.[4] The only such part entrusted
to a bass was the Magician in *Rinaldo* in 1731, when his single aria was
transposed not an octave but a sixth. Two male soprano parts, Alceste
in *Arianna* (composed for a castrato) and Sesto in *Giulio Cesare* (composed for a woman), were later sung by tenors; but on both occasions
Handel supplied almost entirely new music. He usually did the same
when adapting alto parts for tenor (in revivals of *Rinaldo*, *Pastor Fido*,
Scipione, and *Poro*), though here there was no question of octave
transposition. The treatment of Sesto is particularly instructive. The
original soprano part contains five arias and a duet with a contralto.
In the tenor version three of the arias and the duet, one of the most
beautiful pieces in the opera, were cut and three new arias in a different
style inserted. The two arias put down an octave are both vengeance
pieces in C minor where the lower pitch of the voice does no violence
to the music.[5]

It is clear from his practice in revivals that Handel regarded the
castrato voice and the equivalent female voice as interchangeable. Five
parts in *Rinaldo* were sung in different seasons by castrati, and at least
four of them, possibly all five, by women as well.[6] When Handel wrote
for an alto castrato he wrote for an alto first and a castrato second; the
existence in his operas of twenty-six male roles composed for women
tends to confirm this. The pitch is what mattered to him, and for
weighty reasons. Yet in German revivals (almost without exception),
and often elsewhere, the pitch is the one thing ignored.

Various excuses have been made for this. It is said that a woman
playing a man's part is dramatically unsatisfactory. It will be time to
consider this when the Germans allot Cherubino and Octavian to baritones. These are fair parallels, since many of Handel's heroes are represented as young lovers. Moreover, the idea that in an antirealistic con-

---

[4] It is possible that Cleone's aria "Sarò qual vento" in *Alessandro,* a fiery piece
for alto voice, was sung an octave lower by Montagnana (in the part of Clito) in
1732.

[5] There are a few other examples of soprano arias of this type being sung by
tenors, not always in the operas for which they were composed.

[6] Rinaldo in 1713–1715, Goffredo in 1711–1715, Eustazio in 1712, Argante in
1731, the Magician possibly in some of the 1711 performances. Goffredo and Argante
were sung by castrati in 1717.

vention like opera seria we must have realism in the sex of singers, if in nothing else, is an aesthetic absurdity. A modern audience might, it is true, feel some initial surprise at finding military conquerors like Julius Caesar, Alexander the Great, and Richard Coeur-de-Lion portrayed by women. But this is largely prejudice. High voices in such parts are no harder to accept than many other operatic conventions; this is a small thing in comparison with the musical damage wrought by octave transposition, especially in operas like *Rinaldo* or *Giulio Cesare* where, as a result of Handel's fondness for the alto voice, it produces a cast of eight containing one tenor and five basses. That answers a third objection to the use of women: that so many high voices create a monotonous effect. This is simply not true.[7] *Giulio Cesare* is far more likely to jade the ear with five basses than in its original form with two sopranos, four altos, and two basses. That, moreover, is the sound Handel wanted, and to which the entire score is geared.

Whether the orchestration is adjusted or not, octave transposition produces some strange consequences. It is a singular pursuit of verisimilitude—or propriety—that turns Nireno in *Giulio Cesare* into a bass, for he is Cleopatra's eunuch. To transpose the soprano part of Sesto, a young boy, when Handel rewrote it for a grown man in the tenor version, is scarcely less absurd. It also illustrates one of the secondary ill-effects. In the duet with Cornelia at the end of Act I Handel gave the male character the higher part; the substitution of a tenor inverts the parts and alters the intervals. The same situation arises in *Teseo*, *Muzio Scevola*, *Flavio*, *Faramondo*, and *Serse*. Not that the results are much better when the male part is the lower; we then have ungainly maneuvers in tenths and yawning gaps of up to two octaves between the voices.

There are two further overriding arguments against octave transposition, and they explain Handel's aversion to it. In the first place, like all experienced opera composers, he employed the pitch and tessitura of the voice as a primary element in characterization. Each octave has its overtones of color and dramatic weight. A countertenor in "O

---

[7] Except perhaps in the four operas of 1712–1715: *Il Pastor Fido*, *Teseo*, *Silla*, and *Amadigi*, which are almost devoid of natural male voices. But Handel was content to run the risk, and a recent production of *Amadigi* justified him.

Example 42 (*Tamerlano*)

Ter-ra ar-mi   di   sde-gno, mor-rò in - vit - to   e sa-rò for-te,   sa-rò

for -   *- te,*

Isis und Osiris" or a baritone in "Voi che sapete" will demonstrate this
at once: the mellow wisdom of Sarastro and the boyish ardour of Cherubino disappear. Opera seria's association of youth with high voices is
the foundation of Handel's vocal style. The singer provides the driv-
ing power of the opera: he cannot just be fitted into the harmony, as
in the weaker moments of Wagner. Handel's coloratura for tenor and
bass voices is utterly different from his coloratura for altos, whether
castrati or women. Inspection of the tenor part of Bajazet in *Tamerlano*,
or any of the bass parts written for Boschi during the Royal Academy
period, reveals a flexible coloratura ranging over the whole compass of
the voice; its aim is expression, not brilliance (examples 42 and 43). The
coloratura of the Senesino parts composed during the same period has a
much narrower span, often little more than a sixth, and it lies low in the
voice, approximately from middle C up to A or B flat (example 44).
When well sung at this pitch it is expressive and exciting, especially in

Example 43 (*Giulio Cesare*)

Tu   sei il cor   di   que -   - sto co - re,   sei il   mio ben,—— non

t'a -   - di - rar, ——

—————————— non   t'a -   - di - rar!

Example 44 (*Radamisto*)

em_pio ti_ ran - - - - - - - -

- - - - _ *no,*

bravura arias of resolution and defiance. Put it into the lower octave and the gruff rumbling effect is anything but brilliant. If it expresses anything, it is the discomfort of the singer struggling against the grain of the music. It may be heroic of him to try, but it is not the form of heroism prescribed by Handel.

This is difficult to demonstrate conclusively except by appeal to the ear. Those who have heard Janet Baker in the title roles of *Orlando* and *Ariodante*[8] are unlikely to require further evidence. The phonograph supplies some basis for comparison;[9] Russell Oberlin (countertenor), Bernadette Greevy (contralto), Gérard Souzay and Dietrich Fischer-Dieskau (baritones) have each recorded a group of Handel's castrato arias, most of them written for Senesino. The quality of the singing is uniformly high; the musical differences are startling. Oberlin's performance of arias from *Rodelinda* and *Radamisto,* including "Ombra cara,"[10] is outstanding for dramatic conviction, and his ornaments are a model of taste. Souzay also sings, without ornament, one of the finest arias in *Radamisto,* "Perfido, di a quell'empio tiranno,"[11] but the entry of the voice a third below (instead of a sixth above) the unison G of the upper strings, and two octaves below its violin echo, sounds grotesque, and the misplaced coloratura strains the voice. In this scene from

[8] Whether in the theater (Birmingham Barber Institute, conducted by Anthony Lewis) or over the air (BBC Third Programme, conducted by Arnold Goldsbrough).

[9] *Sosarme, Alcina, Rodelinda,* and *Serse* have been recorded complete, with all parts sung at the original pitch. In older German recordings of *Giulio Cesare, Rodelinda,* and *Poro,* and the recent New York *Giulio Cesare,* the castrato parts are sung by baritones.

[10] Example 8, pp. 62–63 above.

[11] Example 44.

the first act, and indeed throughout the opera, the young Radamisto is contrasted with his old father Farasmane, a bass, and his brutal brother-in-law Tiridate, whom we should call a baritone (it is a Boschi part). Tiridate has besieged Radamisto and captured Farasmane, whom he threatens to execute unless Radamisto surrenders at once. "Perfido" is Radamisto's reply, intended to breathe the spirit of youthful courage and defiance. A baritone, however well he sings, is bound to subvert the characterization. He suggests in the idiom of opera seria not a young man but an old man pretending to be young. In its context, with the other two low voices, the effect would be far worse, and in very truth monotonous. Even an artist of the caliber of Fischer-Dieskau, in the arias of the mature Caesar, cannot convey the heroic ring of the music.

The second argument against octave transposition is that it violates the integrity of the music. The texture of a Handel aria is not divisible into separate elements, color, pitch, harmony, melody, and so on. It is conceived as a whole, in precise equilibrium, and the disturbance of one plane reacts upon the rest. This is obvious in arias where the scoring is at once rich and delicate, like Ariodante's "Scherza infida," with its mezzo-soprano voice, muted upper strings, pizzicato basses, and free-ranging bassoons in the middle of the harmony. A baritone here is unthinkable. A whole range of Handel's greatest music falls into this class. But the principle applies throughout the operas. Indeed, while the finest-spun textures suffer conspicuously, because their beauty can be discerned in their ruin, an aria laid out in more orthodox terms, dependent on the correct balance before it can yield its flavor, may be devalued to the commonplace. Not infrequently the voice finds itself below the written bass line, trapped in the nether regions between the cello and the double bass. The color and pitch of every instrument, including the voice, has a positive value that Handel continually exploits. Even when his invention is at its weakest, it is perfectly calculated in terms of texture. The voice is hardly a minor ingredient of an aria; its displacement by an octave is as ham-handed an expedient as the relegation of one of the violin parts in a Haydn quartet to a second cello.

It has been said that a good opera should be foolproof and capable of surviving any number of bad performances. This is a dubious argument at the best of times, and a discreditable one when hauled in to

support laziness or ignorance. But there are two kinds of bad performance: that in which the style and approach are in tune with the music
but the execution is deficient, and that in which the artists, however
technically well equipped, transgress or misrepresent the spirit of the
work. While there have been Handel revivals of both types, the second
is far more damaging and less excusable.

On occasions like this someone is sure to make play with the word
compromise. Opera by its very nature is a gigantic series of compromises, and its realization in performance may involve further adjustments between the ideal and the practicable, a situation that arises
constantly with Wagner. But a compromise between what a great composer desired (provided it is practicable) and what we happen to be ac-
customed to is not a valid artistic operation. It is a piece of intellectual
slovenliness—*Schlamperei*, as Mahler observed in a similar context—and
its fruit is a stunted mediocrity.

There is no denying the precarious nature of the opera seria convention, its narrow basis, and its alienation from later opera. But to
assume, without putting the matter to the test and obtaining conclusive
proof to the contrary, that it will not work today is to presuppose that
it never did work. It ranks with the distasteful and widespread type of
hubris that assumes we know better than their creator how an artist's
work should be performed or displayed—the spirit that gave *King Lear*
a happy ending in the eighteenth century and overpainted nude figures
with discreet drapery in the nineteenth, the spirit of Zeffirelli's *Alcina*
and the Kansas City *Giulio Cesare*. A work of art is not objectively a
success in one period and a failure in another, though its appeal may
vary from age to age. It exists or it does not. We can accept or ignore
it; we have no right to apologize for it and shuffle it forward in alien
plumes, patting ourselves on the back as if we had done it a service.
If its form or idiom is strange, the least we can do is to try to understand it. That means accepting it on its own terms and, in the case of
opera, giving it the best possible chance of coming to life in the theater.
It will then be found, as it invariably is with a great and experienced
creative artist, that the limitations of the convention melt away, like
the wax from which a bronze is cast, and the essential strength remains.

That is after all what has happened in the last hundred years with

Gluck, Mozart, and Verdi. There is no insuperable obstacle, vocal, dramatic, or scenic, to a satisfactory staging of Handel's operas in the modern theater. Brian Trowell, who has directed five of them at the Barber Institute of Fine Arts with no small success, has called him "one of the most underrated figures in the history of opera."[12] Now that Monteverdi is coming into his own, we may go further and call Handel the most underrated of all. He is also the most misrepresented, a state of affairs that a little thought, effort, and humility could easily remedy.

[12] "Handel as a Man of the Theatre," in *Proceedings of the Royal Musical Association 1961/62*, pp. 17–30.

General Index

Aachen, 33
Addison, Joseph, 29
Amadei, Filippo, 40
Annibali, Domenico, 13, 32, 207
Arioso: in opera seria, 8; in H's operas, 42, 51-52, 96, 136, 168, 173, 187, 189, 197
Ariosti, Attilio, 30
Ariosto, Ludovico, 43, 51, 89, 102, 103
Arne, Thomas Augustine, 116
Auber, D. F. E., 81

Bach, Johann Sebastian, 20, 132, 156, 185, 189; Passion settings, 4, 68, 178, 201
Baker, Janet, 211
Baldi (singer), 207
Ballad opera, 28, 32
Ballet: in opera seria, 18; at Haymarket Theatre, 28, 77; at Covent Garden, 33; in H's operas, 33, 38, 43, 51, 53, 77n, 106-107, 129, 131, 142-143, 148, 149, 202; rejected by Metastasio, 56
Beard, John, 34
Beethoven, Ludwig van, 20, 61, 127; *Fidelio*, 15, 60, 69; Eroica Symphony, 20
Beggar's Opera, The, 31
Berenstadt, Gaetano, 207
Bernacchi, Antonio, 207
Berton, Henri Montan, 103

Birmingham, England, H's operas staged at, 143n, 211n, 214
Boito, Arrigo, 37
Bononcini, Giovanni, 1, 30, 38, 157
Borosini, Francesco, 16n, 31
Boschi, Giuseppe Maria, 76, 210, 212
Britten, Benjamin, 14
Burlington, Richard Boyle, Third Earl of, 80
Burlington House, 27
Burney, Charles, 12, 13, 23, 96
Busenello, Giovanni Francesco, 37
Bussani, Giacomo Francesco, 40

Caffarelli (Gaetano Majorano), 33
Calzabigi, Raniero de', 37
Caporale, Andrea, 187
Carestini, Giovanni, 32, 49, 198n, 207
Castrati: in opera seria, 7, 14; popularity of, 15, 29; in H's operas, 15, 28, 31, 69, 114, 116, 117; modern substitutes for, 206-213
Castrucci, Pietro and Prospero, 187, 190
Cavalli, Francesco, 38
Cavatina-cabaletta form, 135-136, 165
Charles I, King of England, 55
Cherubini, Luigi, 83
Chrysander, Friedrich, 3, 51, 55, 127n, 134, 142, 143, 145n, 146n, 150
Cibber, Susanna Maria, 122
Commano, Giovanni, 39
Conti, Gioacchino, 32, 198

215

Continuo realization, 7, 18, 189
Corelli, Arcangelo, 153
Corneille, Pierre, 103, 112
Coro: in opera seria, 8; H's treatment of, 32, 125, 133-134, 147-151
Countertenors, 206-207
Covent Garden Theatre, 33, 102, 142, 202
Cromwell, Oliver, 55
Curtain: use of in 18th century theater, 123-126; H's manipulation of, 126, 128-131
Cuzzoni, Francesca, 12, 31, 39, 40n, 72, 148

Dallas, Texas, 202
Da Ponte, Lorenzo, 12, 37, 53
Dante Alighieri, 56
De Brosses, Charles, 12
Deller, Alfred, 207
Dent, Edward Joseph, viii, 22, 37, 134, 201n
Destouches, André, 38, 82
Deutsch, Otto Erich, 28n, 41n
Donizetti, Gaetano, 107, 206
Dotti, Anna, 23
Dresden, 133
Drottningholm, 203
Dryden, John, 57
Dublin, 122
Durastanti, Margherita, 40

Edwards, Miss (singer), 34
Eisenschmidt, Joachim, viii, 41, 43n, 101, 102, 123, 124n, 137, 159, 204
Elpidia (pasticcio opera), 31
Embellishment. See Ornamentation
Euripides, 72, 73
Exit arias: opera seria convention, 8-10, 36, 126, 129; exceptions to rule, 9, 29; H's treatment of, 20, 52, 127, 133, 144-146; increased in Bononcini's Serse, 38

Farinelli (Carlo Broschi), 32
Farncombe, Charles, 201n
Faustina Bordoni, 12, 31, 39, 40n, 72, 148
Fischer-Dieskau, Dietrich, 211, 212
Fitzwilliam Museum, Cambridge, 171n

Francesina (Elizabeth Duparc), 34
Freud, Siegmund, 11, 96

Gasparini, Francesco, 140n
George I, 30
George II, 30, 199
George III, 102
Germany, H's operas revived in, 2, 200-201, 208
Gluck, Christoph Willibald, 6, 7, 23, 24, 37, 132, 147, 157, 178, 214; "reform" of opera, 7, 14, 57; Alceste, 60, 73; Orfeo ed Euridice, 83, 96
Goldsbrough, Arnold, 211n
Göttingen, 200
Greevy, Bernadette, 211
Grout, Donald, 61, 127

Hagen, Oskar, 200, 201, 202
Halle, 25, 200, 202
Halle edition (of H's works), 3, 38, 128, 201
Hamburg: H's career at, 25-26; style and influence of opera at, 26-27, 186
Handel Opera Society (London), 201n
Hanoverian dynasty, 100
Hasse, Johann Adolf, 57
Haydn, Joseph, 20, 212
Haym, Nicola Francesco, 37, 40, 41, 72
Haymarket Theatre, 28, 77, 133. See also King's Theatre
Heidegger, John James, 31, 33, 40
Hill, Aaron, 28, 29
Homer, 56
Houdar de la Motte, Antoine, 38
Huntington Library, California, 27n

Jennens, Charles, 41
Johnson, Samuel, 5
Jones, Inigo, 56n, 125
Jonson, Ben, 56n

Kansas City, 202, 213
Keiser, Reinhard, 26, 186
Kimbell, David, 37n
King's Theatre in the Haymarket, 30, 33, 37, 38, 124. See also Haymarket Theatre

Knapp, J. Merrill, 37n
Kytch, Jean Christian, 186

Leichtentritt, Hugo, viii
Leipzig, 202
Lewis, Anthony, 152n, 211n
Loewenberg, Alfred, 121
London: H's operas composed for, 11, 27-35; old librettos modified for, 37-43
Lully, Jean Baptiste, 37, 147

Machines. *See* Transformation scenes
Mahler, Gustav, 213
Mainwaring, John, 126
Marchi, Antonio, 43n
Mayr, Simone, 103
Méhul, Etienne Nicolas, 103, 132
Metastasio, Pietro: "reform" of opera seria libretto, 5, 7, 56-57, 81, 168; H's settings of, 39, 57-59, 72, 131, 141, 148, 149, 168; mentioned, 103, 107, 115
Meyerbeer, Giacomo, 18, 57
Milton, John, 57, 103
Minato, Niccolò, 116
Montagnana, Antonio, 32, 39, 42, 76, 91, 208n
Monteverdi, Claudio, 7, 13, 23, 37, 108, 121, 214; *The Coronation of Poppea*, 27, 38, 60, 107, 109
Morell, Thomas, 151
Mozart, Wolfgang Amadeus, 7, 13, 17, 20, 23, 24, 37, 38, 53, 101, 109, 121, 126, 127, 128, 157, 165, 205, 206, 214; *The Magic Flute*, 7, 46, 91, 97, 210; *Così fan tutte*, 7, 12, 121; *Idomeneo*, 7; *Don Giovanni*, 12, 117; *The Marriage of Figaro*, 115, 117, 121, 208, 210; *Die Entführung aus dem Serail*, 149; piano concertos, 158n; concert aria "Misera, dove son?" 161
Munich Opera, 201
Muratori, Ludovico Antonio, 41

Neapolitan School, 31, 35, 115, 116, 156. *See also* Vinci, Leonardo
New York City Opera, 203n
Nicolini (Nicolò Grimaldi), 191, 207
Novosielski, Michael, 124

Oberlin, Russell, 207, 211
Opera of the Nobility, 32, 33
Orlandini, Giuseppe Maria, 31
Ornamentation, 4, 10, 17-18, 201-202, 205-206, 211
Overture: in opera seria, 8; H's treatment of, 58, 130-132

Pacini, Andrea, 207
Palmerini (singer), 39
Partenio, Giovanni Domenico, 113n
Pasticcio operas, 13, 27, 31, 33
Pergolesi, Giovanni Battista, 31
Piovene, Agostino, 140n, 145n
Porpora, Nicola Antonio, 32
Powers, Harold S., 1n, 38n
Prince of Wales (Frederick, son of George II), 33, 102, 149
Puccini, Giacomo, 6
Purcell, Henry, 28, 153

Quantz, Johann Joachim, 206
Quinault, Philippe, 37

Racine, Jean, 103
Rameau, Jean Philippe, 21, 102, 147
Reinhold, Henry Theodore, 34
Rich, John, 33
Ristori, Giovanni Alberto, 13
Ritornello, H's treatment of, 47, 51, 156-167 *passim*, 173, 205
Riva, Giuseppe, 40, 41
Robinson, Michael F., 100n
Rolli, Paolo, 37, 40, 41
Rome, restrictions on opera at, 15n, 25, 26
Rossi, Giacomo, 28, 29, 37
Rossini, Gioachino, 107, 108, 206; *L'Equivoco stravagante*, 15; *The Barber of Seville*, 115
Royal Academy of Music, 15, 30, 31, 34, 39, 40, 41, 72, 76, 111, 130, 178, 191, 199, 210

Sallé, Marie, 33, 77n
Salvi, Antonio, 106, 143
Sammartini, Giuseppe, 187, 198
Sartorio, Antonio, 40
Savage, William, 34, 206

Scarlatti, Alessandro, 37, 107, 153, 157;
    Tigrane, 186
Scenery in 18th century theatre, 77, 123-
    128, 204
Schoenberg, Arnold, 18
Schubert, Franz, 36, 152, 165
Scribe, Eugène, 57
Senesino (Francesco Bernardi), 31, 32,
    40, 148, 199, 207, 210, 211
Shakespeare, William, 15*n*, 55, 60, 61,
    103, 121, 136, 150, 213
Sheppard, F. H. W., 124*n*
Simile arias: in opera seria, 9, 10; H's
    treatment of, 22, 76, 137; multiplied
    by Metastasio, 59
Southern, Richard, 123*n*
Souzay, Gérard, 211
Spontini, Gasparo, 18
Stampiglia, Silvio, 38
Steele, Sir Richard, 29, 77, 78*n*
Steglich, Rudolf, 38
Stockholm Opera, 202
Strada del Pò, Anna, 32
Strauss, Richard, 6, 208
Streatfeild, R. A., viii

Terry, Ellen, 21
Transformation scenes, 18, 28, 29, 30, 32,
    77-81, 124-125, 184, 203; rejected by
    Metastasio, 56-57, 81
Trowell, Brian, 214

Valentini (Valentino Urbani), 207
Venice: operatic tradition in, 9*n*, 23, 27,
    38, 42, 56; *Agrippina* composed for,
    26; old Venetian librettos reset by H,
    35, 40, 72, 111, 116; *Alcina* revived at,
    202
Veracini, Francesco Maria, 55
Verdi, Giuseppe, 3, 7, 13, 17, 34, 37, 121,
    126, 214; *Otello*, 36, 60, 132, 203; *Il
    Trovatore*, 56; *Ernani*, 56; *Simon Boc-
    canegra*, 60; *Macbeth*, 203
Vienna, 133
Vinci, Leonardo, 13, 31

Wagner, Richard, 4, 6, 7, 13, 18, 168,
    204, 210, 213; *The Ring*, 19, 97; *Sieg-
    fried*, 36; *Lohengrin*, 103; *The Flying
    Dutchman*, 125, 201; *Tristan and
    Isolde*, 136
Waltz, Gustavus, 34
Watteau, Antoine, 194
Weber, Carl Maria, 81; *Oberon*, 81;
    Euryanthe, 103
Wolff, Helmuth Christian, viii, 202

Young, Cecilia, 34

Zeffirelli, Franco, 202, 203, 213
Zeno, Apostolo, 5

Index of Handel's Works

OPERAS

Admeto, 15, 22, 24, 60, 72, 73, 80, 124, 125, 127, 131-132, 196, 197

Agrippina, 9, 23, 26, 27, 37, 39, 42, 72*n*, 107-111, 115, 134, 144, 146, 152, 153*n*, 171, 176, 189, 190; modern revivals, 202; quoted, 110-111, 112, 153

Alcina, 11, 15, 22-23, 33, 34, 41, 43-53, 59, 82, 83, 89, 102, 115, 137, 142, 143, 147, 149, 159, 164, 167, 168, 190, 205; modern revivals, 202, 203, 213; recordings, 53, 211*n*; quoted, 44, 45, 46, 48, 50, 52

Alessandro, 31, 55, 133, 134, 141*n*, 148, 159, 164, 176, 177, 198, 208*n*

Almira, 26, 39, 61, 106, 107, 129, 156, 157, 173, 178, 190*n*, 192, 196

Amadigi di Gaula, 11, 16, 29, 32, 38, 72*n*, 77*n*, 80, 82, 88, 89, 125*n*, 136, 140, 147, 150, 158, 169, 191, 209*n*; modern revivals, 209*n*; quoted, 88, 90, 192

Arianna in Creta, 33, 81, 125*n*, 130, 142, 149, 153, 173, 176, 190, 194, 208; quoted, 154-155

Ariodante, 3*n*, 11, 27, 33, 34, 39, 42, 59, 81, 102-106, 114, 125, 127, 137, 142-143, 147, 149, 164, 169, 189, 191, 196, 198, 201*n*, 212; modern revivals, 211; quoted, 104, 105

Arminio, 27, 61, 132, 141*n*, 150, 161, 165-166, 194, 198

Atalanta, 33, 42, 55*n*, 100, 102, 124, 134, 149, 165

Berenice, 27, 42, 132, 137, 141*n*, 150, 167, 186

Deidamia, 11, 15, 59, 116, 128, 131, 142, 167-168, 196, 199; modern revivals, 201

Ezio, 3*n*, 15*n*, 32, 39, 42, 57-59, 73, 131, 137, 149, 159-161, 165, 178, 190, 191, 194, 201*n*; quoted, 160

Faramondo, 10, 33, 56, 132, 141, 149, 159, 168, 197, 198, 206, 209

Flavio, 11, 22, 30, 41, 81, 102, 103, 111-114, 136, 140, 164, 199, 209

Floridante, 26*n*, 81, 127*n*, 135, 141, 169, 199

Giulio Cesare in Egitto, 3*n*, 11, 14, 22, 31, 42, 54, 60, 61, 64, 68, 72, 124, 127, 128, 131, 133, 134, 141, 147, 148, 169, 177, 184, 191, 194, 196, 199, 208, 209; modern revivals, 200, 201, 202-203, 209, 213; recordings, 203*n*, 211*n*; quoted, 182-183, 193, 210

Giustino, 10, 33*n*, 39, 81, 116, 125, 132, 140, 149, 156, 160*n*, 173, 176, 190, 191, 196, 197, 198*n*; quoted, 174-175

Imeneo, 34, 115, 116, 121, 122, 127, 135, 141*n*, 142, 150, 176, 186, 187

Lotario, 16*n*, 31, 32, 41, 42, 55, 72, 128, 133, 135, 137, 147, 164, 177, 178, 199

Muzio Scevola, 209

Orlando, 22, 24, 32, 55*n*, 72*n*, 80, 83, 89, 91-97, 102, 115, 136, 137, 140, 141, 147, 149, 161, 167, 169, 178, 189, 190, 197; modern revivals, 211; quoted, 92-93, 94-95, 98-99, 138-139, 162-163, 170

Ottone, 41, 81, 141, 177, 199

Partenope, 15, 27, 31, 32, 102, 114, 115, 132, 134, 189, 191, 199

Pastor Fido, Il, 13*n*, 41, 55*n*, 102, 127, 142, 147, 153*n*, 171, 189, 191, 196, 198, 208, 209*n*

Poro, 13, 16*n*, 32, 39, 42, 55*n*, 57-59, 73, 76, 125, 132, 141, 149, 150, 164, 168, 176, 194, 196, 208; recordings, 211*n*; quoted, 195

Radamisto, 15, 30, 41, 60, 61, 64, 72, 115, 127, 128, 134, 137, 147, 148, 165, 166-167, 168, 186, 187, 190, 191, 194, 198, 199, 207, 211-212; recordings, 211; quoted, 62-63, 65, 66-67, 188, 211

Riccardo Primo, 30, 55, 72, 100, 132, 134, 176, 177, 178, 190, 191, 198, 199

Rinaldo, 9, 11, 12, 28, 29, 32, 37, 41, 55*n*, 69, 77-80, 81, 82, 107, 124*n*, 125, 129, 147, 186, 189, 190, 191, 198, 208; modern revivals, 191*n*, 209

Rodelinda, 16*n*, 31, 41, 60, 64, 69, 81, 103, 128, 135, 140, 141, 147-148, 164, 169, 171, 178, 190, 198; modern revivals, 200; recordings, 211; quoted, 172

Rodrigo, 11, 26, 27*n*, 39, 69, 147, 158, 169, 186; quoted, 72

Scipione, 56, 72, 130, 137, 140, 165, 178, 208

Serse, 2, 3*n*, 9, 15, 35, 38, 39, 40, 106, 116-121, 128, 137, 149, 165, 168, 169, 176, 177, 189, 209; modern revivals, 200, 201, 202; recordings, 211*n*; quoted, 1, 118, 119

Silla, 11, 27, 61, 69, 80, 81, 129, 137, 147, 171, 176, 187, 191, 209*n*

Siroe, 15, 39, 42, 57-59, 132, 178, 186

Sosarme, 11, 32, 73, 114, 122, 132, 133, 147, 149, 167, 196; recordings, 76, 211*n*; quoted, 74-75

Tamerlano, 11, 14, 16*n*, 22, 23, 31, 39, 55, 59, 60, 64, 68, 95, 101*n*, 115, 135, 140, 141, 144-147, 150, 158, 159*n*, 167, 168*n*, 178, 189, 190, 191, 198*n*, 199, 203, 210; quoted, 70-71, 179, 180-181, 210

Teseo, 29, 37, 72, 79, 82, 83, 129, 134, 147, 171, 187, 190, 199, 209; quoted, 84-85, 86-87

Tolomeo, 13*n*, 55*n*, 132, 141, 147, 169, 176, 178, 189, 194, 196

OTHER WORKS

Aci, Galatea e Polifemo, 29*n*, 73

Acis and Galatea, 30, 102

Allegro ed il Penseroso, L', 103

Athalia, 173

Belshazzar, 41

Cantatas, 25-26, 143, 153

Church music, 25

Coronation Anthems, 186

Esther, 30

Hercules, 24, 72, 83, 136, 198

Israel in Egypt, 5

Jephtha, 64*n*

Joshua, 59

Messiah, 5, 69, 83

Oratorios, 4-5, 19, 24, 25-26, 33, 34, 115, 151, 186, 196

Organ concertos, 34

Resurrezione, La, 69, 153*n*, 186

Saul, 81, 116, 127

Semele, 34, 72

Solomon, 32, 103, 199

Susanna, 32, 103, 199

Terpsicore, 196

Theodora, 81, 151